HALL OF FAME
BASEBALL

HALL OF FAME
BASEBALL

MAC DAVIS

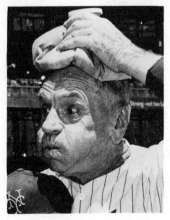

COLLINS
WORLD

Published by Wm. Collins + World Publishing Co.
2080 West 117 Street, Cleveland, Ohio 44111
Published simultaneously in Canada by
Nelson, Foster & Scott Ltd.
Library of Congress catalog card number: 72-9966
Copyright © 1975 Mac Davis
Photo Credits—United Press International
ISBN 0-529-05062-5 (Trade Edition)
ISBN 0-529-05063-3 (Library Edition)
Designed by Jacques Chazaud

CONTENTS

FOREWORD

According to legend, the game of baseball was invented by a famous American Civil War general named Abner Doubleday. It was he who in 1839 laid out the first baseball field, in Cooperstown, New York. There the Hall of Fame now stands as a shrine for all the immortals of the game.

According to fact, big-league baseball began in 1876 with the formation of the National League. It was composed of all the professional teams, and all the players signed season-long contracts.

Since then, millions of men of all ages have played baseball, but up to now only about fifty thousand players have been able to break into the big leagues for their fame and fortune. Of all these ballplayers, fewer than two hundred have gained the supreme honor which baseball bestows upon its greatest players—enshrinement in the National Baseball Hall of Fame. The legendary titans now in the Cooperstown shrine are the true immortals of baseball.

This book offers a matchless gallery of thirty-three Hall of Fame immortals—the most remarkable and most magnificent figures now glorifying the home of baseball's demigods. They tower above all the other Hall of Fame immortals.

Not only did these chosen thirty-three accomplish the greatest heroics and achieve the most incredible feats for the glory of the game, but more than all the other Hall of Famers, they enriched America's national pastime with thrills, drama, glamour, humanity, humor, lore and legends.

In thirty-three colorful and intimate profiles, baseball fans of all ages are offered an intriguing meeting with the most monumental figures now in the Hall of Fame and an exciting glimpse into their fabulous careers.

Here they are in all their glory for a brief companionship with all who love the game of baseball. They are all worth meeting and knowing well. For never will the deeds and feats of these thirty-three Hall of Fame supermen be overshadowed by any other immortals in baseball history.

MAC DAVIS

LEGEND OF THE HALL OF FAME

In the peaceful village of Cooperstown, nestling amidst the rural beauty of central New York State, there is a sports institution which is unlike any other in the world. It is the National Baseball Hall of Fame and Museum. Why and how did Cooperstown with a population of only 2,500 souls become the site for a shrine glorifying the greatest immortals of America's national pastime?

It all began on December 30, 1907, when a special commission of seven prominent men, all friends of the baseball game, and who had been appointed by the club owners of the sixteen major-league teams then in existence, released a most important report to the entire baseball world. It announced that "the first scheme for playing the game of baseball, according to the best evidence obtainable, was devised by Abner Doubleday at Cooperstown, New York, in 1839." Abner Doubleday is famous in American history as the soldier who fired the first Union gun in defense of Fort Sumter, at the start of the bloody Civil War between the states.

For years there had been a widespread belief in the baseball world that the game deserved a shrine to glorify its greatest heroes. The

1907 special-commission report motivated the plans for the establishment of a National Hall of Fame in Cooperstown, the birthplace of baseball.

In 1939, the National Baseball Hall of Fame and Museum became a reality. It was quartered in a newly built, Colonial-style, red-brick building in Cooperstown at the head of Main Street. However, this original building which housed the world's most complete collection of the game's memorabilia was soon outgrown and additions had to be made and dedicated, doubling the size of the facility.

At a centennial celebration held on June 12, 1939, in a colorful ceremony, organized baseball formally dedicated the Hall of Fame. On that historic day, Judge Kenesaw Mountain Landis, the first Baseball High Commissioner in history, made the chief dedicatory address. He remarked in part:

It is fitting that baseball should have a National Museum. And nowhere else than its birthplace could this museum be appropriately situated. To the pioneers who were the moving spirits of the game in its infancy, and to the players who have been elected to the Hall of Fame, we pay just tribute. I now declare the National Baseball Hall of Fame and Museum in Coopers-town, New York, the birthplace of baseball, officially open. May it forever stand as a symbol of clean play and good sportsmanship.

The National Baseball Hall of Fame and Museum is now extremely rich in priceless possessions and relics covering almost the entire gamut of baseball history, lore and legends. In the museum, there is fascinating baseball memorabilia of all types on exhibit — bats, gloves, uniforms, shoes, balls, trophies, jewelry, lockers, paintings, sculptures, drawings, photographs and even ball-park seats — all forming a classic and graphic history of the game's greatest yesteryears. The museum's valuable collection covering the history and development of baseball in America is so vast that not all the priceless relics can be displayed at the same time.

The Hall of Fame now houses the largest baseball library in the world. It is a repository for thousands of baseball books, publications, valuable documents, ancient contracts, and more than one hundred motion picture films on baseball. The Hall of Fame library is a research haven for historians, scholars, writers and students.

Though every cranny of the National Baseball Museum is crammed with fascinating exhibits, the most popular place in the Cooperstown shrine is the Hall of Fame wing of the Museum. Here the real immortals of the game are enshrined. Here hang the bronze plaques with suitable inscriptions honoring baseball's best.

Ever since 1936, baseball's outstanding experts — the members of the Baseball Writers Association of America, each with at least ten years standing in the profession — have been engaged annually in the serious and important task of selecting the baseball heroes worthy of inclusion in the Hall of Fame.

To be eligible for election to the Hall of Fame a player must have played actively in the major leagues at some time during a period beginning twenty years prior to the annual election, and ending five years prior to the election. He must also have played in each of ten championship seasons. Players have been chosen for Hall of Fame honors on the basis of ability, integrity, sportsmanship, character, and their contributions to the teams on which they played, and to baseball in general. Any player receiving seventy-five percent of the vote in the annual election promptly and officially gains honored-membership to the Hall of Fame. In recent years, more than a thousand baseball experts from the Baseball Writers Association of America have voted in the annual election for their Hall of Fame favorites.

Old-timers who have been retired from the major leagues for more than twenty-five years are chosen for Hall of Fame membership by an eminently qualified special Veterans Committee comprised of baseball officials who have given long and meritorious service to the game.

The first five baseball players who were voted into the Hall of Fame when it first opened its golden portals were the game's most fabulous titans: Ty Cobb, Babe Ruth, Honus Wagner, Christy Mathewson and Walter Johnson. At the last count, the total membership of the National Baseball Hall of Fame numbered 138.

The biggest and most joyous day of each year in Cooperstown is Hall of Fame Day, for it is the supreme moment for the game's greatest living players. Usually in July, the newly elected Hall of Famers are inducted in a colorful ceremony staged on the porch of the National Baseball Library before a huge crowd of visitors gathered from all over the United States to witness this important event.

On this great day, two major-league teams, one from each circuit, are always given the special honor of playing an exhibition game on Doubleday Field, just a block away from the Hall of Fame, where Abner Doubleday first played baseball so long ago.

Every year now at least 250,000 people from all over the world make the pilgrimage to the charming rural village of Cooperstown to visit the National Baseball Hall of Fame and Museum. Here, memory speaks of baseball's greatest heroes who are the wonders of the game — of the most magnificent feats ever achieved by the titans of big-league baseball, of once-fought incredible diamond battles, and of unsurpassed events from the past. In the Hall of Fame shrine lives the drama, romance, lore and legend that shaped big-league baseball into America's national pastime.

OUTFIELDERS

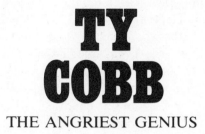

TY COBB

THE ANGRIEST GENIUS

BORN: Tyrus Raymond Cobb
      December 18, 1886, Narrows, Georgia
DIED: July 17, 1961, Atlanta, Georgia
HEIGHT: 6'¾"   WEIGHT: 175 lbs.
Threw right-handed and batted left-handed
Lifetime batting average (24 years): .367

O f the tens of thousands of men who have played major-league baseball since it began, no star sparkled for so long and with such glitter as the fabled Tyrus Raymond Cobb, known as the Georgia Peach. Even as the 1970's roll on, no player appears to be even within striking distance of some of the records Ty Cobb set during his twenty-four legendary years in the big leagues.

It was no wonder then, that when the Baseball Hall of Fame was set up at Cooperstown, New York, Cobb was the very first player elected. He always was in a class by himself.

Ty Cobb was born in the small Georgia town of Narrows in 1886. From his early childhood his parents had lofty plans for his future. His father was a well-to-do state senator, a newspaper publisher and a professor. Young Ty was expected to study for a career in law or medicine, or the military.

But from early boyhood he had an insatiable desire to play baseball, and though he had won appointments to both West Point and Annapolis, the rebellious young man shocked his parents by becoming a professional baseball player.

3

Cobb played only one year in the minors before his contract was sold to the Detroit Tigers for a paltry $700. In August, 1905, at the age of eighteen, he became a center fielder in the major leagues.

It wasn't easy at first, even though Cobb almost immediately began swinging a hot bat. But these were the frontier days of baseball, and the players were tough and hard-boiled and particularly aggressive against rookies. In self-defense against the hazing, Cobb turned into a mean, bitter, hot-tempered rebel, the angriest man in baseball. He became the most volatile, the most daring and the fiercest competitor baseball ever had. He also became the most hated player of all time.

Cobb challenged opposing players, his own teammates, his bosses, newspapermen, umpires and even heckling fans. He became so irascible that none of his teammates would room with him. He had fist fights on and off the field, and with spikes slashing, he dug his way across big-league diamonds, leaving a legion of enemies behind.

Wherever he played, he aroused such violent hatred that he often needed police protection. Once he almost killed an umpire in a fist fight under the stands. Another time, an angry fan attacked him with a knife, and once a mob of irate fans tried to lynch him. But without fear, he marched alone to the highest peaks of baseball glory.

His unbelievable talents outweighed all the travail brought on by his belligerence. In a short time he established himself as the most spectacular fielder, base stealer and hitter in the game. In the field he roved center field as well as anybody who ever played and he had a rifle arm. On the bases, he stole almost at will, flashing his spikes and spilling more infielders' blood than any other competitor in history. At times, after reaching first, he would score by stealing second, third and home. Seven times he stole four bases in a game. One year he stole 96 bases in a 154-game season, and six times he led his league in stealing. In all, he stole 892 bases in his lifetime, the modern-day record.

But it was at the bat that Cobb really terrorized his rivals. He had the keenest of hitting eyes, incredible coordination and tremendous speed. A left-handed hitter with a curious choke grip on the bat, he belted the ball into left field, pulled it to right or hit straightaway as he wished. He was unsurpassed as a bunter, and whenever he did bunt, it was almost always a safe hit.

He was able to turn a game around every time he came up. He created such tension in the opposing team that he set the terms of the game. He upset pitchers, catchers, infielders and outfielders alike. For they knew that he was safe if they made the slightest bobble.

In 1907, Ty Cobb won his first batting championship with a .350 mark. Thereafter, he led the American League in batting for an unprecedented twelve years — nine of them in a row. He batted .400 or better three times and for an incredible span of twenty-three years in a row he hit .300 or higher.

Playing in an era of faraway fences, "dead" baseballs and spitballs and beanballs that were everyday hazards to the hitter, only Ty Cobb ever made five or more hits in a game fourteen times. Only he ever collected 3,052 singles, scored 2,224 runs and wound up with a lifetime career total of 4,191 hits. No other major-league player ever approached 4,000.

He was the only player in history ever to appear in 3,033 big-league games, coming to bat 11,429 times. And the most incredible record of all — his lifetime batting average over his long career of .367 — is likely never to be broken.

There were scores of other records too, for when he quit the game in 1928 at the age of forty-two (and still able to hit .323), there was little doubt that he had left his indelible mark on the game. In all, he left ninety different baseball records, many of them still on the books.

The greatest all-around baseball player of all time grew mellow in his retirement. Once the game's most evil-tempered genius, and baseball's most hated player, he tried to recast his notorious image into a more admirable man of good deeds. Ty Cobb built a hospital in his hometown. He set up endowment funds to help the needy. He chartered an educational foundation to give free scholarships and financial aid to worthy college students.

Lonely, unhappy, and afflicted with several diseases, he died at the age of seventy-four. But the last days of the legendary Georgia Peach were sweetened somehow with the knowledge that all his-. torians considered him as the Number One baseball player of all time.

Curiously, even in death, the fantastic Ty Cobb still amazed the baseball world, for he had left behind him a fortune of more than eleven million dollars. He became the richest big-league ballplayer in history.

NEVER ONE LIKE HIM AGAIN

BORN: George Herman Ruth
February 6, 1895, Baltimore, Maryland
DIED: August 16, 1948, New York, New York
HEIGHT: 6'2"   WEIGHT: 215 lbs.
Threw and batted left-handed
Lifetime batting average (22 years): .342

In the twenty-two glorious years Babe Ruth played in the major leagues, he gained wealth and immortality beyond the dreams of most men. But he gave the game more than he took from it. For more than any other player in history, the Babe won for baseball its place of honor as America's national pastime. He was responsible for lifting the game to a popularity it had never known before. Of all the players installed with reverence in the Hall of Fame, the Babe is by all odds the best-known and most beloved.

But Babe Ruth's start in life hardly presaged such a magnificent career. He was born George Herman Ruth and as an infant lived in a shabby room over his father's saloon on the Baltimore waterfront. From childhood he was neglected by his parents, who had no time or affection for the lad. Often they beat him without mercy.

Before he was seven years of age, his mother died in a fire. Later, his father was murdered in a street brawl. The youngster was on his own and became an incorrigible. He ran wild on the slum streets; he stole, chewed tobacco, drank whiskey and fought with police. Before

7

he was ten, for his own salvation, he was sent away to St. Mary's Industrial School for Boys. It was a refuge for orphans and the homeless as well as a prison for juvenile delinquents — actually a reform school. Babe spent the better part of his teen-age years there.

He was supposed to be learning the trade of a tailor, but Babe was always more interested in playing ball. When he was only twelve, he was catching and pitching for the school team, made up mostly of sixteen-year-olds. At sixteen, he was the star pitcher for St. Mary's varsity, and he usually struck out seventeen hitters a game.

Tall, gangling Ruth became such a skilled left-handed pitcher for the reform school that, when he was eighteen, he was offered a job pitching professionally for the Baltimore Orioles, a topflight minor-league team. He could hardly believe his good fortune.

"You mean somebody is crazy enough to want to pay me six hundred dollars a season just to play ball?" he asked in bewilderment.

To him it was all the money in the world. He'd have played for nothing because of his love for the game. In order to get him freed from the reform school, the Baltimore owner and manager had to adopt the youngster and become his legal guardian. That's why his teammates nicknamed him the Babe.

He was astonishingly good in the minors, winning twenty-two games for Baltimore, and before the year was out, he was in the big leagues pitching for the Boston Red Sox. And for twenty-one years thereafter, he was to remain one of the most formidable players in history.

The Babe wasted no time getting on the road to greatness. In his first three full seasons in the big leagues, he established himself as one of the best pitchers of the period by winning sixty-four games. In five seasons, he helped his team win three pennants and three World Series championships. In winning three games in the classic, he set a record of twenty-nine consecutive scoreless innings — a record that stood for more than forty-five years.

Ruth might well have been one of the great all-time pitchers if he hadn't carried such a big bat. When, in 1918, pitcher Ruth hit eleven home runs to lead the league, his team captain, outfielder Harry Hooper, began to pester the Red Sox manager to shift Ruth to the outfield so that he could play every day in every game.

"You must be out of your head to think I would do anything like that," the manager roared. "If I took the best pitcher in the league and made him an outfielder, I'd be the laughingstock of the game."

But the manager finally relented, and winning southpaw Babe Ruth became slugging outfielder Babe Ruth. Baseball lost a great pitcher but gained the greatest home-run hitter of all time. And, to no one's surprise, Ruth also became one of the finest right fielders in history.

At the end of the 1919 season, after outfielder Ruth had amazed the baseball world by hitting twenty-nine homers, the financially pinched Red Sox sold him to the rich New York Yankees for $125,000 in cash and a loan of $350,000. For Babe Ruth, it was the turning point of his career.

In 1920, big-league baseball was blackened with a shocking scandal. It was revealed that eight famous players of a pennant-winning team had "thrown" the 1919 World Series — for a price. Baseball fell to an all-time low in public esteem, and it almost died as the American national sport.

Ironically, it was Babe Ruth, the once incorrigible delinquent rebel who had spent the greatest part of his youth in a reform school, who saved baseball. In the wake of that infamous "Black Sox" scandal, he rescued the game from ruin with his oversized bat, his epic heroics, his vital personality, his infectious joy and his lovable ways. Babe Ruth lifted big-league baseball to a national popularity unheard of before then. Because of his home runs, he became better known on the national scene than the president of the United States. He came to be adored by countless millions of people from all over the world. No other athlete in history ever gained such a grip upon the affections of so many millions of youngsters as the Bambino did when he was pioneering the era of the home run.

Curiously, at the zenith of his fame as the King of Swat, the Babe was not built like an athlete nor did he even resemble a ballplayer. His roly-poly body, 240 lbs. of it, stood on absurdly spindly legs with ankles as slim as a girl's. He ran with mincing steps. But when he smashed the ball, there was nothing mincing about that.

He swaggered wildly through his baseball life and he overdid everything. But everything the Babe did was majestic. No one before or since has ever belted such awesome and satisfying home runs. He set a pace for "firsts" and "mosts" unlike anyone else, and his home runs worked a revolution in the game, changing its whole character.

Whether he homered or fanned, Babe did it with such gigantic and exuberant gusto that it made all gasp with wonder. He was the only player in history for whom the crowd cheered even when he struck out. For a Ruthian strikeout was an unforgettable thing to see. He struck out 1,330 times all told, but he so intimidated pitchers that they walked him 2,056 times.

Babe Ruth was the first player ever to crack out 50 or more home runs in a single season three times. He was the only player who ever slugged 40 or more homers a season eleven times. He was the first to hit 60 homers in a season, and he did it in only 151 games. He walloped 2 or more homers in a single game seventy-two times, another all-time mark. Twelve times he was the home-run champion of his league. And his fabulous lifetime record of 714 home runs stood for almost forty years after he set it.

His slugging wasn't restricted to gargantuan home runs. He was also one of baseball's most consistent hitters. In 8,399 times up, he made 2,837 hits, scored 2,174 times, and compiled a lifetime hitting average of .342, which is among the top six in the history of baseball. His fantastic total of 2,229 runs-batted-in breaks down to an average of more than 100 a year, including his pitching days and his tail-end seasons.

Those remarkable statistics are only part of the story. His very presence in the ball park was electrifying and though he reached his peak in the twenties and thirties, he brought joy to people during boom times and brought solace to people in depression times. He was paid $80,000, more than the president of the United States, one year, but even the millions of people out of work then did not begrudge him his good fortune. He had become a hero to the masses. To the poor, the wretched, the underprivileged and the neglected, he was a shining inspiration. He had come so far from such a low state.

With the profits of success, Ruth turned his life into one glorious spree. He played hard and he lived hard. On and off the field he was equally exciting, a fantastic celebrity always besieged by a worshipping public. His universal fame earned him a fortune of several million dollars. But he always had a big grin and a ready, warm handshake for everybody, especially for the kids.

When, in 1935, he was discarded by the New York Yankees, he played out the string as a spare outfielder for the Boston Braves. Then he hung his spikes up for good, a fat, weary forty-year-old. The King of Home Runs ended his glorious reign with sixty-one major-league records in the books, and among them were twenty-eight World Series marks.

On the evening of August 16, 1948, the Babe, now a bedridden victim of cancer, spoke his last words. He climbed out of bed and stood proud and erect. The alarmed nurse asked him where he was going.

The Babe smiled: "I'm going over the valley." And so he died.

His body lay in state in Yankee Stadium. More than 100,000 fans filed past his coffin to see the Big Guy for the last time. Twice as many came to his funeral to bid him farewell. And throughout most of the world, millions mourned for the most colorful, most glamorous, most famous and most lovable baseball player who ever lived.

Time will never dim the roaring legend of Babe Ruth.

JOE DiMAGGIO

A YANKEE JOLTER

BORN: Joseph Paul DiMaggio
  November 25, 1914, Martinez, California
HEIGHT: 6'2"   WEIGHT: 193 lbs.
Threw and batted right-handed
Lifetime batting average (13 seasons): .325

Joe DiMaggio is generally regarded as baseball's greatest center fielder. His phenomenal playing in thirteen years of major-league competition sparked the New York Yankees to ten American League pennants and eight World Series championships. He became one of the youngest baseball greats to be enshrined in the Hall of Fame.

Born the eighth child to an Italian immigrant fisherman, Joe DiMaggio at an early age had firmly decided not to follow his father's trade on the wharves of San Francisco. By the time he was twelve he already knew what he wanted to be — a big-league baseball player. His stern father scoffed at his ambition; but with the help of an understanding mother and an older brother, Joe became a professional baseball player at the age of eighteen. He accepted an offer to play with the San Francisco Seals of the Pacific Coast League.

Joe's older brother Vince had been responsible for the offer. Vince was already with the Seals and the club was in need of a shortstop. The elder DiMag persuaded the manager to give his kid brother Joe a tryout. Almost immediately, Joe convinced the Seals that he was not

only a fair shortshop but also an outfielder of unsurpassed skills and a
hitter of supreme power and consistency. In his first year in baseball
he set an astonishing minor-league record by hitting safely in sixty-
one consecutive games. He also hit twenty-eight homers and wound
up with a .340 batting average.

Big-league scouts went wild over him and almost every major-
league team wanted to sign him. Fantastic offers were coming in for
his purchase. But hardly had the 1934 season begun when Joe
suffered a severe knee injury and had to spend several weeks with the
knee in a splint. This scared off a good many of the major-league
clubs who then considered him a bad risk. But in 1936, when Joe was
twenty-one, the New York Yankees took a chance. They bought his
contract from the Seals for $25,000.

From his rookie season in the majors to his last day in the World
Series of 1951, DiMaggio was a spectacular star. He became the
heart and soul of the fabulous Yankees. He became one of baseball's
picture hitters, a paragon of fielding ability and a perfect base runner.
Fans never had seen a more graceful center fielder than the Yankee

Clipper, as he came to be known. With his smooth, casual style he speared fly balls in deepest center field for spectacular putouts. His arm was so strong and so accurate that he cut down a host of base runners and scared many more into not trying to steal extra bases.

Despite a burned foot which kept him out of action for the first few weeks of his freshman season, he hit for an average of .323, with twenty-nine home runs among his 209 hits.

The following season, the stamp of greatness was really applied to Joltin' Joe. He became a baseball hero for a whole nation. Millions idolized him. In that second year he belted out 46 home runs, batted in 167 runs and had a rousing .346 batting average.

His heroics in the years to come exceeded even these figures. (One year he batted .381 and in another .352, both good for the league batting championship.) But none of his incredible feats equaled the fantastic record he set as a hitter during the 1941 season. He set a record that year which will endure longer than any other all-time record in the annals of the game. It may never be matched.

On May 15, 1941, in a game against the White Sox, Joe singled. And from that day on, he continued to hit safely in every game the Yankees played until he went hitless in a game played on July 17 against the Cleveland Indians. During that phenomenal streak, he had hit safely in fifty-six consecutive games, pounding out ninety-one hits in 223 times at bat (a .408 clip). He had registered fifteen home runs, batted in fifty-five runs, and had crossed the plate fifty-six times.

Even after that incredible streak had ended, Joe wasn't through. The very next day he started another consecutive-game hitting streak. That one lasted through sixteen games. Thus, the Yankee Clipper wrote into the history books an almost unbelievable record. He became the only player ever to hit safely in seventy-two out of seventy-three consecutive big-league games.

On the strength of his many fantastic seasons, DiMaggio became the first player in history to be paid a salary of $100,000. Yet it was ironic that he was never lucky as a ballplayer. Injuries and physical ailments dogged him through his career. And at his peak (at the age of twenty-eight) he left the majors for three years to serve with the United States Armed Forces in World War II.

When he returned in 1946, he was instrumental in leading the Yankees to four more World Series championships before his retirement after the 1951 season.

He left behind a legend of consistency matched by no other. In his thirteen seasons with the Yankees he collected 2,214 hits, 361 homers, 1,390 runs batted in, 1,537 runs scored and a lifetime batting average of .325. He led the league at least once in runs, triples, homers and batting average, which earned him (on three occasions) the coveted honor of Most Valuable Player of the American League.

In 1951, when Joe was thirty-seven years old, he finished his career by doubling in his last time at bat in the World Series. After that, he said that he could no longer produce his best as a top player. And although the Yankees offered to continue his $100,000 salary no matter how few games he played, the most graceful center fielder the game ever saw turned his back on the offer and retired. No player ever departed from the major leagues a more respected or more beloved man than proud Joe DiMaggio. He was more than perhaps the greatest center fielder of all time. He was a symbol of his generation and a legend in his lifetime.

MEL OTT

BOY IN A MAN'S WORLD

BORN: Melvin Thomas Ott
        March 2, 1909, Gretna, Louisiana
DIED: November 21, 1958, New Orleans, Louisiana
HEIGHT: 5′9″   WEIGHT: 170 lbs.
Threw right-handed and batted left-handed
Lifetime batting average (22 years): .304

As a little boy, Mel Ott used to sit and fish on the banks of the Mississippi River. He never dreamed that some day near that very spot a Mel Ott Park would be dedicated. He never dreamed that one day he would be enshrined in the Hall of Fame as one of the most devastating sluggers big-league baseball has ever known.

That spot on the Mississippi River was Gretna, Louisiana, where Mel was born in 1909. It was across the river from New Orleans. Mel put on his first baseball glove and swung his first little bat when he could barely toddle. With the help of his father and an uncle, the boy developed rapidly. Before the age of sixteen, he was already catching for a fast semipro team owned by a wealthy New Orleans lumberman who happened to be a close friend of John McGraw, the fabled manager of the New York Giants.

So it was that on a September morning in 1925, a stocky, baby-faced country boy, clutching the handle of a cheap cardboard suitcase that contained all his worldly possessions, arrived at the Polo Grounds, home of the Giants. He timidly knocked at the office door

of Manager McGraw, the man who had just won four consecutive National League pennants.

As he entered the little office, the boy, in a quavering voice, said: "Mr. McGraw, I have a letter here from Mr. Williams in New Orleans. He said I should see you about a job with the Giants. My name is Mel Ott. I'm a catcher."

McGraw looked him over, up and down. Mel stood barely 69 in. tall, weighed less than 160 lbs. and looked like a sixteen-year-old, which he was.

Although he thought his friend was playing a joke on him, the amused manager allowed the youngster to work out with the Giants the next day. From that day on, Master Melvin, as the sportswriters sometimes called him, was a member of the New York Giants and he compiled a record that included 511 home runs, which at the time he retired twenty-two years later, was a National League record.

His accomplishments were achieved as an outfielder, for McGraw saw immediately that Ott was too small to catch and that his already heavy legs would tend to become muscle-bound with the constant crouching behind home plate. As the Giants' right fielder, Ott became as polished at that position as anyone who had ever played it. He played with such skill that he became widely known as Mr. Right Field.

When Mel Ott was only seventeen, he was already hitting .383 and at nineteen he had already become famous as one of the mightiest sluggers in the game. That season he hit .328, pounded out forty-two home runs and drove in 151 runs.

The hard-boiled McGraw watched over his boy wonder with the gruff tenderness of a loving father with a favorite son. Once when he spotted him playing in a friendly poker game with some of the veterans of the team, he growled at Mel angrily: "I'm fining you one hundred dollars. You're still too young to be playing cards with grown men."

When Mel Ott finally reached his twenty-first birthday and could consider himself a full-grown man, he was already a full-fledged big-league veteran with almost five major-league seasons behind him.

As the years went by and baseball's boy wonder grew older, he set a sizzling pace for the game's leading home-run sluggers. In eight different seasons, he belted 30 or more homers. He hit 2 home runs in a single game, forty-nine times. During his twenty-two-year run as a Giant hero, he smashed 511 home runs.

So feared a batter was Mel Ott that he set the all-time National League record for most bases on balls — 1,708. On ten occasions he led the league in walks, with 100 or more bases on balls per season.

The chunky little right fielder collected a bushel of records as a big leaguer. He became the first modern player to score six runs in a single nine-inning game. He accomplished that astonishing feat twice. He was walked five times in a single game on four occasions.

He played in 2,730 games, made 2,876 hits, scored 1,859 runs, and drove in 1,860 runs. Also, he was the first National League player in history to reach the 500-homer mark for his fame.

Baseball's first and greatest boy wonder climaxed his many glorious playing years in the majors by becoming the manager of the New York Giants. He was a beloved pilot.

He was thirty-nine when he finally retired from major-league action. But in 1958, cruel fate caught up with this legendary figure who had already been enshrined in the Hall of Fame. Mel Ott was fatally injured in an automobile accident. He was no more than forty-nine when he died.

But his legend endures as an inspiration for every boy with a big-league dream. In Mel Ott's hometown of Gretna, just outside of New Orleans, there is now a beautiful park dedicated in his honor. The Mel Ott Park helps keep green the memory of one of baseball's greatest heroes.

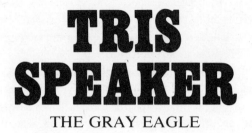

TRIS SPEAKER

THE GRAY EAGLE

BORN: Tristram Speaker
    April 4, 1888, Hubbard City, Texas
DIED: December 8, 1958, Lake Whitney, Texas
HEIGHT: 5'11½"   WEIGHT: 193 lbs.
Threw and batted left-handed
Lifetime batting average (22 years): .344

A product of the Texas plains, Tris Speaker as a boy rode horses, roped cattle, and was an excellent marksman. Though naturally right-handed, he became a left-hander at the age of ten when he was thrown from a bucking horse and broke his collarbone and right arm. While still in his teens, he was a fine rodeo performer. However, what he wanted most to be was a baseball player.

He was barely seventeen when he began to pitch professionally for a baseball club in the North Texas League, for fifty dollars a month. However, he was a failure as a southpaw hurler. Discouraged, he gave up pitching and became an outfielder.

He was twenty when the Boston Red Sox plucked him out of bush-league obscurity and brought him into the limelight of the big leagues. Tris Speaker made the most of it. He remained in the major leagues for twenty-two years and distinguished himself as the greatest defensive glove man ever to play center field.

No one in baseball history ever patrolled center field more daringly, more efficiently, and with greater scientific judgment than

fleet-footed Tris, who became known as the Gray Eagle. Somehow he always knew where a hit ball was going to fall.

He was a magician in the outfield, playing his center-field position so shallow that he was practically an extra infielder for his team. This enabled him to rob batters of sure hits driven behind second base or short. There was no such thing as a safe Texas League single when Tris Speaker roamed the outfield. Moreover, no center fielder in history ever went back with such lightning speed to spear a long fly to the outfield as did the Gray Eagle making impossible catches over his shoulder.

His total of 449 assists has never been matched by a major-league outfielder. In two separate seasons, he recorded 35 assists for his fame and it is still an all-time record. Nine different times he led the majors in chances accepted by an outfielder and his lifetime totals of putouts (6,706), assists (449) and chances accepted (7,195) are records not likely ever to be equaled.

In addition to his fielding prowess, the brawny Texan with powerful hands and a voice like rolling thunder also carved his niche in big-league history as one of its greatest hitters.

Only Tris Speaker ever pounded out as many as 793 doubles during a major-league career. In 10,208 times at bat, he slashed out 3,515 safe hits, scored 1,881 runs, and wound up with a lifetime batting average of .344. He also stole 433 bases.

Although twice sparking the Boston Red Sox to the world baseball championship, Tris Speaker was traded to the Cleveland Indians in 1916 because of a salary dispute. Eventually he became their playing manager. In 1920, while batting a lofty .388, he piloted the Indians to their first pennant and World Series championship.

At the age of forty the Gray Eagle was still flying high in the majors, still getting his hits, and still patrolling the outfield with all of his glove wizardry.

When the Hall of Fame came into existence, it was not surprising that one of the first major-league players chosen to enter there was the legendary Tris Speaker, who began his baseball career as a miserable failure, but who with dogged determination and matchless skills climbed to the highest peaks of big-league glory.

TED WILLIAMS

THE MIGHTY SPLINTER

BORN: Theodore Samuel Williams
    August 30, 1918, San Diego, California
HEIGHT: 6'4"   WEIGHT: 198 lbs.
Threw right-handed and batted left-handed
Lifetime batting average (19 years): .344

Since 1941, no batter in baseball ever has hit better than .400. It isn't likely that anybody ever will again. But that year, the man who did it was a cocky, twenty-three-year-old outfielder for the Boston Red Sox, Theodore Samuel Williams, and he became only the seventh player in the history of baseball to pass that lofty mark.

Williams, in his third year in the majors, came tearing down the stretch of 143 games and reached the final day of the season still at .400. The Red Sox had a doubleheader scheduled to complete their season.

"Look, Ted," said his considerate manager. "You can sit out both games today if you want to protect your .400 hitting average."

"Oh, no," said Ted Williams. "I'm playing today. If I'm going to be a .400 hitter, I'll be one for the whole year. I won't sneak into it. I want to have more than my toenails on the line."

And so he played in the last two games, making six hits in eight times at bat and compiling a season average of .406!

Anyone who knew Ted Williams could have predicted that that

would be his decision. He grew up in San Diego, California, as brash and confident as any youngster who ever put on a baseball uniform. Though his mother, a bonneted Salvation Army worker known as Salvation May, wanted him to join the noble cause of saving souls, Ted wanted to play ball. He lived, slept and ate baseball.

He was still a junior at San Diego High School in 1936 when he dropped out of school to play professional baseball for the San Diego Padres of the Pacific Coast League. He earned $150 a month and was supposed to be a lefty pitcher. But wiser heads saw him at the plate and immediately turned him into a left fielder. For what those wiser heads saw was one of the greatest hitters in baseball history.

Williams played two years at San Diego learning his trade and then reported to the Red Sox in spring training in 1938. Though he was not yet twenty, he had some idea of how good a hitter he was. He was overbearing, arrogant, headstrong and high-strung and he made no bones about the fact that he was going to be the greatest hitter in the majors. He made so much noise about it that the Red Sox manager shipped him back to the minors.

When the irritated and relieved veteran Red Sox outfielders heard the news, they gave young Ted a riding: "So long, fresh busher, you're going just where you belong." But Williams sneered back at them: "Look, you baboons, I'll be back before you know it, and I'll be making more dough than all of you combined." In time, he did precisely that.

After leading his league, the top minor league at the time, with a cool .366 and hitting forty-three home runs, Williams was back at the Red Sox training camp in 1939. As a freshman big leaguer, he hit .327, belted thirty-one homers and drove in 145 runs, the best in baseball. He was acclaimed Rookie of the Year. And that was only the beginning.

In nineteen subsequent playing years, Williams was a spectacular hitter. He had probably the keenest eyes in baseball history and would not go for a pitch if it were a shade out of the strike zone. As a result, he was a continuous threat to opposing pitchers who often teased other hitters into going for bad pitches. Ted just waited — and then teed off.

In 1942, just before he left for three years of military service in World War II, Williams not only won the American League batting championship with a .356 mark, but also captured his first triple crown. He was first in hitting average, first in home runs and first in runs-batted-in. Later he won a second triple crown of the majors — the rarest of big-league feats.

But despite Ted's heroics on the field, he was never a completely popular ballplayer. Cocky and self-assured, he made public displays of temper and often alienated crowds by refusing to tip his hat in response to their adulation. He never gave autographs. Few men in baseball ever triggered as many feuds as the man they called the Splendid Splinter. He had a distressing habit of bluntly saying what was on his mind, no matter who might be offended.

Baseball's most reluctant hero then became a fighter pilot in the United States Marine Corps. When he returned in 1946, he resumed his position as the greatest hitter of his time. He not only set a major-league record in runs scored (142), but also hit thirty-eight home runs, batted .342 — and sparked the Red Sox to a pennant, becoming the Most Valuable Player of the year. He won that honor again in 1949.

That was the year he displayed a side of himself few people knew. Johnny Orlando was the clubhouse attendant for the Red Sox and Williams was a particular favorite. It is the custom of big leaguers to tip the clubhouse attendant at the end of the season. But no player ever gave the attendant so great a tip as Williams gave Orlando at the end of the 1946 season, the only time Ted was in a World Series. He endorsed his full check for the World Series, $2,140.89, over to Johnny.

Meanwhile on the field he was still the most terrifying hitter in baseball. Pitchers walked him more than 100 times in each of eleven seasons. Twice he was walked 162 times in a single season. Once he was walked in nineteen games in a row and another time he got on base 16 consecutive times. Next to the mighty Babe Ruth, he drew more bases on balls than any other player in history: 2,018.

Then at thirty-four, Williams got his second call to military duty. The Marines called him back for the Korean War. In that conflict he flew an F-9 Panther jet for thirty-nine combat missions. During one mission his plane was hit by enemy guns and Captain Williams found himself in an aircraft ripped apart and on fire. But always the cocky and confident one he did not bail out. Miraculously, he belly-crashed the blazing plane and scrambled out uninjured.

He returned to the Red Sox in 1954 and spent seven more years endangering the lives of rival pitchers. Despite injuries (broken collarbone, chipped elbow, infected heel, pulled muscles, slipped disk) he continued to hit at an amazing pace. In 1957 at the age of thirty-nine, he walloped thirty-eight home runs and batted an amazing .388 to capture his fifth American League batting championship. He was the oldest player ever to win a big-league batting title. Then he won another at age forty in 1958.

On September 26, 1960, when Williams was forty-two years old, he played his last major-league game. He went out with a grand flourish. In his last hurrah as a big leaguer, Williams hit 29 homers, compiled a .317 batting average and in his final time at bat in the majors, he clouted the longest home run he had ever hit. He closed out a fabulous major-league career with 521 home runs and a lifetime batting average of .344.

As a rookie, Williams sometimes confided in friends that his only goal in life was to become famous. "I want to walk down the street one day and have people say, 'There goes the greatest hitter that ever lived.' "

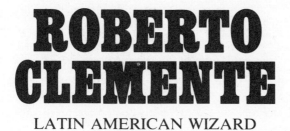

ROBERTO CLEMENTE

LATIN AMERICAN WIZARD

BORN: Roberto Walker Clemente
        August 18, 1934, Carolina, Puerto Rico
DIED: December 31, 1972
HEIGHT: 5' 11"   WEIGHT: 185 lbs.
Threw and batted right-handed
Lifetime batting average (18 years): .317

O f all the baseball elite now enshrined in the Hall of Fame, Roberto Clemente is unique in his glory. In 1973, he became the first Latin American baseball player to enter the Hall of Fame, and the only player in history to have the rules waived to admit him only a few months after his untimely death at age thirty-eight.

No Hall of Fame immortal ever departed from this world in a more heroic or nobler way than Roberto Clemente. On the rainy New Year's Eve of 1972, he flew off on a mission of mercy, to help others in misfortune by taking relief supplies to the victims of an earthquake in Nicaragua. His plane crashed into the sea, and he perished in his noble effort. The waters swallowed him, and his body was never found. So, tragically ended the fabulous baseball career of a superstar and a rare human being.

For Clemente it all began in the Puerto Rican town of Carolina where he spent his boyhood dreaming of fame as a sports hero. In his teen-age years, he was an outstanding high school athlete, playing baseball and starring in track. He was so versatile as a track-and-field

29

performer that he hoped to gain fame in the Olympic Games. But one day, while Clemente was still a high-school boy, the owner of a professional baseball team in Santurce saw him play in an amateur baseball game. The owner was so impressed by his diamond skills that he persuaded Clemente to accept a bonus of $500, and become a pro baseball player for his team, at a munificent salary of sixty dollars a month. He became an instant sensation in the pro ranks.

But Clemente's destiny was not to remain an obscure small-time baseball wonder in Puerto Rico. For before long, he was spotted by a big-league scout who was so impressed by his spectacular playing that he persuaded him to accept a $10,000 bonus and sign a major-league contract to play for the then Brooklyn Dodgers. Roberto Clemente was all of nineteen years old then.

With high hopes, he left his native Puerto Rico to play baseball in Canada with the Montreal team, the Dodgers' top farm club. He was shipped there to acquire some seasoning for the big leagues. But somehow, the Dodgers ignored his potential greatness as an outfielder and let him slip away from them to the Pittsburgh Pirates who bought his contract for only $4,000. Clemente was twenty-one years old then.

As soon as he came to the big leagues he blossomed into one of the most magnificent players ever seen in major-league competition. No one ever patrolled a right field with greater efficiency and brilliance than fleet-footed Clemente. Nobody ever speared fly balls quite like he did. His leaping catches and astonishing throws were breathtaking in every game he played. He was an exciting player for big-league glory, both on defense and attack, with glove and bat.

During his eighteen glorious years in the major leagues, although he often suffered from various physical ailments, he played in 2,433 games and won four National League batting championships and a Most Valuable Player award. Twelve times he was honored with the coveted Golden Glove award for his outstanding fielding skills. At bat, he was equally magnificent. He hit over .300 in thirteen different seasons. He collected 3,000 safe hits and became the eleventh baseball great in history to achieve this rare batting feat. He wound up with a .317 lifetime batting average for his fame.

Roberto Clemente was more than a superstar of the majors. He was an inspiring leader to his teammates, always with a deep concern for others. Three times he sparked the Pittsburgh Pirates to pennants, and twice he inspired them to World Series championships. With glove, bat and fighting spirit, he dominated every World Series classic he played in. In his last World Series, he was more magnificent than ever before, even though at the time he was thirty-seven years old. That 1971 post-season classic went down in history as the "Clemente World Series," for almost single-handed, he won the world championship for his team, with his twelve hits which included two doubles, a triple and two homers. Never was Roberto Clemente more idolized as a baseball hero than he was at thirty-seven, after his heroics in the 1971 World Series.

But the Clemente legend came to a sudden and tragic end on that rainy New Year's Eve in 1972, when his concern for the welfare of others moved him to fly off on a mission of mercy.

Although Roberto Clemente perished in the effort, it was his final journey to glory — for his immortality as a baseball player and a noble man.

STAN MUSIAL

MAN FOR ALL SEASONS

BORN: Stanley Frank Musial
   November 21, 1920, Donora, Pennsylvania
HEIGHT: 6' WEIGHT: 180 lbs.
Threw and batted left-handed
Lifetime batting average (22 years): .331

When Stanley Frank Musial was called up by the St. Louis Cardinals late in the season of 1941, he was not yet twenty-one. Yet he swung into big-league action as an outfielder with such ease that in his first half-dozen years in the majors, he was voted Most Valuable Player of the National League three times, won three batting titles with such gaudy figures as .357, .365 and .376 and sparked the Cardinals to three pennants and two World Series championships.

Stan Musial made those early years look so easy that one would guess that he was just fulfilling his destiny. Yet only two years before he arrived in the majors, he was so discouraged by his failure as a left-handed pitcher that he came perilously close to quitting the game.

In fact, Musial nearly never got the chance to play the game at all. Born in the coal town of Donora, Pennsylvania, the son of a poor Polish-immigrant laborer, Musial had a dream of becoming a professional ballplayer. But his father adamantly insisted that his eldest boy stay in school and forget about "wasting your life on a foolish game played by children."

When Stan received an offer of a pitching job with a minor-league club, he was still under eighteen and he needed his stubborn father's permission to sign. The old man said no. Stan pleaded and begged with his father and the argument ran on. Finally the youngster broke into tears, blubbering like a baby. That did it. Moved by his son's tears, Papa Lukatz Musial, in tears himself, said: "For my boy I wanted a better life than I have had. But if baseball means this much to you, I won't stand in your way. This is a free country, and you are free not to go to college."

But there was an even higher obstacle ahead. While working as an insignificant pitcher in the minors, Musial fell one day and dislocated his left shoulder, his pitching arm, thus ending his hurling career. There he was at nineteen, an unwanted, sore-armed pitcher with no job, no money and no place to go. In addition, he had a wife to support, for he had married his high school sweetheart.

"I guess I'll have to quit baseball," Stan told his manager.

"You will not," said his manager. "Just because you can't pitch is no reason to leave the game. I'll make an outfielder out of you. You can hit, I know that. You still can make it big."

The fatherly minor-league manager who encouraged the disheartened youngster was Dickie Kerr, once a major-league pitcher. He had Stan move into his home to live with him, freeing him from financial worries during the awkward period when he was switching from pitcher to outfielder. Stan Musial never forgot the helpful manager who started him on his way to glory. When a son was born, Musial named the child Richard Kerr Musial. And years later, when Musial had become famous and wealthy, he still did not forget his benefactor. In 1958, Stan presented him with a handsome new house in his hometown, secretly bought by Stan as a gift for Kerr's sixty-fifth birthday.

Stan Musial's professional conversion from pitcher to outfielder was rapid. He soon became a swift, sure-handed and graceful gardener, and of course, he was a devastating hitter. Stan was forced to withstand ridicule by teammates and rival players who laughed at his peek-a-boo stance at home plate. They said he held the bat like a fly swatter.

Nevertheless, he didn't change it, and soon that stance became the most menacing one in the National League. And as the seasons went by, he was described by experts as being technically as scientific a hitter as Ty Cobb — the highest accolade.

For twenty-one years in a row he played in 100 games a season. He set the all-time National League record for durability by playing in 895 consecutive games. He played in more major-league games than any player in history: 3,026. He went to bat a record 10,972 times and only he played more than 1,000 games at each of two positions, outfield and first base.

So despite his unorthodox batting stance, for seventeen years Musial hit .300 or better, knocking in the most runs (1,951), scoring the most times (1,949) and hitting more doubles (725) than any other player in National League history.

But he did even more as a fantastic slugger. Musial alone, of all the hitters in history, hit five home runs in one day, a doubleheader in 1954. He clouted 475 homers in his career. And he surpassed all players in history for extra-base hits, winding up his career with 1,377. As for total bases, he amassed the unbelievable number of 6,134.

In all, Musial, the Man as they called him around the league, won seven National League batting championships and finished with a .331 lifetime batting average.

Stan the Man was a strange hero, beloved by fans and players and even umpires. To the youth of America he was a model person. At the height of his fame, he was still so modest that he was embarrassed when the Cardinals boosted his salary to $100,000 a season.

"I would have played for less," he said shyly, "but they wanted me to have it to show their appreciation."

When it was all added up, after the twenty-second season as a Cardinal, his baseball earnings reached more than a million dollars.

No one deserved it more, for when he finally quit the field at the ripe old age of forty-three, he owned more than sixty major-league and National League records. He was welcomed into the Hall of Fame with loving arms in 1969, the first year he was eligible. It is there that he belongs, for the ages.

MICKEY MANTLE

SWITCH-HITTER TERROR

BORN: Mickey Charles Mantle
   October 20, 1931, Spavinaw, Oklahoma
HEIGHT: 6'   WEIGHT: 201 lbs.
Threw right-handed, batted left-handed and right-handed
Lifetime batting average (18 years): .298

When Mickey Mantle was born, his happy father, a zinc and lead miner in Oklahoma who once had been an obscure semipro pitcher, made a bold and rash prediction.

"This boy of mine will become a famous big-league baseball player," he told all who would listen to him. And Charles "Mutt" Mantle wasted no time before starting to prepare his newborn son for a baseball career. Mickey was only six months old when he wore his first baseball cap, knitted by his mother. At three, he wore his first baseball uniform, tailored from a pair of his father's old baseball uniform pants. Before he was five, Mickey was given his first baseball glove. When he was six, his ambitious father began to teach him how to catch a baseball and hit it with a bat. Mickey was an apt pupil and a quick learner. For endless hours throughout his boyhood he practiced the art of baseball, and no boy ever tried harder to please his father. The fear of failing in his father's eyes plagued Mickey throughout his youth.

As the boy grew older, he became a strong and muscular lad, and because he lived in football country, he became a star halfback for the

Commerce High School football team. During one fierce high school football game, Mickey was kicked in the leg. To his horror, he soon discovered that his injured leg was afflicted with a rare bone disease called osteomyelitis. There was no more football playing for Mickey Mantle. But there was still baseball.

When Mickey graduated from high school, his father convinced a baseball scout for the famed New York Yankees that he was worth a bonus of $1,100 to be signed up as a professional ballplayer with a big-league future in sight. At seventeen Mickey became a pro baseball shortstop for the Yankees' farm club in the Kansas-Oklahoma-Missouri League, at a salary of $140 a month.

In his first eighty-nine pro games, he made 49 errors. But he was a terror at the plate, hitting baseball pitches left-handed and right-handed with equal power.

He was nineteen when he finally was called up by the New York Yankees to play in the big leagues. Scared, shy and bewildered, Mickey Mantle came to the majors as a typical hayseed from the sticks. He wore a cheap, ill-fitting suit and a straw hat and carried a four-dollar cardboard suitcase with all his worldly belongings in it. Moreover, he came to the major leagues afflicted with chronic osteomyelitis of the left leg and a fear that because of it, any game he played in might prove to be his last.

Mickey made his big-league debut as a hard-hitting, fleet-footed center fielder, but though he came up to the majors in a flood of praise and was hailed as an instant star, by the middle of his first season he had slumped so far down that he was shipped back to the minors. It was a devastating humiliation for that blond, muscular country boy who had been dedicated to big-league fame by his ambitious father.

However, when the downhearted and discouraged Mickey Mantle expected sympathy from the man he loved and respected the most, instead, his father told him man to man:

"There's no use feeling sorry for yourself. If you want to grub for a living in the mines like I've been doing, come home. Crying won't get you back into the big leagues, but guts will. If you've got the courage and ambition to go on playing your best, you'll make it back to the majors and stay there!"

Just one month later, Mickey was back in the big leagues, playing center field for the New York Yankees, and he began to tear apart his magnificent powerful body with his dedicated zeal to achieve baseball greatness. His father, who became a victim of cancer, lived long enough to see Mickey have a spectacular first season as a shining big leaguer. Rookie Mantle hit .311 and belted twenty-three home runs to help the Yankees win a pennant. And in his first World Series Mickey delivered ten hits, including two homers. It was the beginning of a glorious career for a center fielder who became one of the greatest of all time.

Mickey Mantle's glory road was paved with years of pain, frustration and struggle, for he suffered many injuries, and six times had to undergo major surgery on both legs so that he could continue to play. Nevertheless, he performed monumental feats for his fame.

In 1956 he became the ninth player in history to win the coveted Triple Crown of the majors, for being tops in batting, home-run hitting and runs-batted-in. That memorable season he won the batting championship with a .353 average, batted-in 130 runs, and belted 52 homers.

Time and again, he led his league in slugging, fielding averages, and bases on balls. He became the most feared and most devastating switch-hitter the majors ever had. Many of the home runs which he hit left-handed and right-handed for long distances had to be seen to be believed. He became the only switch hitter in baseball history to hit as many as 536 homers from both sides of home plate.

Despite all the crippling injuries which he suffered through the eighteen seasons he starred for the New York Yankees, he played in 2,401 major league games — more than any other Yankee player in history ever accomplished, and he collected 2,415 safe hits, scored 1,677 runs, batted-in 1,509 runs and stole more than 200 bases.

So versatile a performer became Mickey Mantle in the big leagues that three times he was honored with the coveted Most Valuable Player award. And so fabulous and popular he became as a major-league star that he was the first player in history to be paid a season's salary of $100,000 for six consecutive years.

With his matchless courage, magnificent fielding and awesome hitting, he sparked the New York Yankees to twelve pennants in his first fourteen seasons in the major leagues. And he became the only player in World Series history to hit as many as eighteen home runs for his fame.

At the end of the 1968 season, when the thirty-seven-year-old, injury-scarred and pain-weary Mickey Mantle finally hung up his spikes as a big-league player, he was a living baseball legend.

In 1974, at the age of forty-three, the incredible Mickey Mantle had his last "hurrah" as a super baseball great, and he completed his long journey to the baseball immortality his father had predicted for him. He was enshrined in the Cooperstown Hall of Fame, ever to be honored and remembered as one of the greatest immortals of the game.

INFIELDERS

LOU GEHRIG

THE IRON HORSE

BORN: Henry Louis Gehrig
June 19, 1903, New York, New York
DIED: June 2, 1941, Riverdale, New York
HEIGHT: 6'1"   WEIGHT: 212 lbs.
Threw and batted left-handed
Lifetime batting average (17 years): .340

Lou Gehrig, whose strength and durability had amazed the world of athletics for fourteen consecutive baseball years, was stricken with an insidious and crippling disease called amyotrophic lateral sclerosis at the age of thirty-six. It made him a paralyzed invalid and his strength and life slowly trickled away.

But before he died, there was a memorable Lou Gehrig Day at New York's famed Yankee Stadium. More than 80,000 fans came to express their admiration, affection and love for the famous athlete who was facing a slow death. It was a day of cheers and tears, the most emotional event in the history of the national pastime. Hardened old players and young fans alike cried without shame. Then Lou Gehrig, tears in his eyes, walked to the center of the diamond to speak briefly to the hushed crowd.

"Fans," he said, "they tell me I've been given a bad break. But I've played baseball with the greatest teammates a ballplayer could ask for, and I've had my share of good things in life. With all the good I've had today, I consider myself the luckiest man on the face of the earth."

It was more than "luck" however, which made Henry Louis Gehrig the most admired athlete of his generation. He made his own luck. Long before he entered the Hall of Fame he achieved a diamond greatness known by few men in the history of the game.

He was born in the Bronx, New York, of humble origin, the son of a handyman and a domestic. He began to play baseball in the streets of the city. His German immigrant parents held high hopes for him. They envisioned him as an architect. But instead of building houses he became a professional baseball player and he built a legend for the ages.

Husky young Lou was still a student at Columbia University,

scoring in football and baseball, when fate forced him to make an important decision that shaped his destiny. A serious illness beset his father and money was desperately needed for an operation and hospital care. Gehrig dropped out of college to accept an offer from the New York Yankees to play pro ball. He got a bonus of $1,500 and signed for a salary of $3,000 a year.

Sent off to a Yankee farm club in the Eastern League to acquire experience, Gehrig in the beginning was a crude, clumsy and graceless first baseman. His first manager declared that he was a big oaf who couldn't field, hit or do anything else. But the industrious youngster worked hard, never stopped trying to learn, polished his fielding and improved his hitting in his years in the minors and was ready when the big club called him up to the big leagues in 1925.

On the memorable afternoon of June 2 of that year, veteran Wally Pipp, the Yankees' regular first baseman reported to the ball park with a headache. The Yankee manager excused him for the day and said, "I'll give that big kid Gehrig a chance to play first and we'll see what he can do."

What Gehrig did was stay in the Yankee lineup as the regular first baseman for the next fourteen years!

He set a pace for durability, endurance and consistency that never will be equaled. Without interruption, every day in every game, season after season, he played first base despite broken fingers, broken thumbs, fractured toes, torn leg muscles, wrenched shoulders and back, chipped elbows and severe lumbago attacks to establish himself as the most indestructible ball player in history. He played in 2,130 consecutive major-league games, perhaps the most incredible record of all time.

During that long playing streak, he accepted 20,598 fielding chances, made 19,511 putouts, 1,087 assists and only 194 errors. Season after season, he paced the American League in runs, in total bases and in amazing feats. He became the first player in the twentieth century to hit four consecutive homers in a nine-inning game. He was the only major leaguer in history to smash 23 bases-loaded home runs. For twelve years in a row he hit over .300 and he batted in more than 100 runs in each of thirteen seasons. Seven times he batted in more than 150 runs, including an unbelievable 184 driven in during the 1931 season.

He hit more home runs than any other first baseman in history, 497; and among his 2,721 hits were 535 doubles and 161 triples. He scored 1,888 times, batted in 1,991 runs and walked 1,510 times. He compiled a lifetime batting average of .340!

As a four-time winner of the American League's Most Valuable Player Award, Larrupin' Lou, as they called him, helped the Yankees win no less than seven pennants. In thirty-four World Series games, he made forty-three hits for a .361 batting mark.

The famed Iron Horse of Baseball was more than a phenomenal first baseman. He was a hero of the finest personal habits and his character was beyond reproach. Though modest and taciturn, almost always avoiding the limelight, he gained a popularity accorded to few baseball greats. He became a national idol and an inspiration to the youth of America.

On May 2, 1939, minutes before that afternoon's game was to begin, the Yankees' captain and first baseman Lou Gehrig walked up to the umpire-in-chief and handed him the team's batting order for that game. The ump glanced at it casually. Then suddenly his eyes widened and his mouth popped open with surprise. For he didn't see the name of Gehrig written in on the batting order for that game.

"What's up, Lou?" asked the astonished umpire. "Aren't you playing first base today as usual?" He quickly stopped asking questions and turned away, for he saw Gehrig shaking his head sadly, tears flowing from his eyes.

The startling news that Lou Gehrig had stopped playing first base for the Yankees spread throughout the baseball world before that game was over. The most unbelievable baseball record ever achieved by a major-league player was done. The legendary Iron Horse had come to the end of his fantastic playing streak — 2,130 consecutive games.

Not long after, the doctors revealed to a shocked baseball world the nature of Gehrig's terminal disease that was eating away his life. He never played baseball again.

His locker at the Yankee Stadium was turned into a shrine and his famed "Number 4" which he had worn on his baseball uniform was retired forever. In a touching tribute to the glory and greatness of Lou Gehrig, Hollywood filmed a motion picture based on his life and career for the whole world to see.

Born in June of 1903, he died in June of 1941, at the age of only thirty-eight. The whole nation grieved for the tragic Lou Gehrig. But he had lived long enough to see himself enter the Hall of Fame as a never-to-be-forgotten baseball immortal.

GEORGE SISLER

POETRY IN MOTION

BORN: George Sisler
       March 24, 1893, Nimisila, Ohio
DIED: March 26, 1973, Richmond Heights, Missouri
HEIGHT: 5'10½"   WEIGHT: 170 lbs.
Threw and batted left-handed
Lifetime batting average (16 years): .340

W hen twenty-one-year-old George Sisler, a graduate of the University of Michigan, where he had excelled in football, basketball, and baseball, came to the big leagues as a pitcher for the St. Louis Browns of the American League, he nearly caused a war between the two major leagues because the Pittsburgh Pirates also claimed him. Nevertheless, after a bitter dispute between the two leagues over the rightful possession of the modest, soft-spoken, self-effacing, and gentlemanly George Sisler, he remained with the St. Louis Browns and showed instant promise of becoming one of the greatest hurlers in the game. In the first few games that handsome rookie southpaw hurled in the majors, he outpitched the outstanding hurlers then in his league. But surprisingly, George Sisler lasted only twelve games as a winning major-league pitcher.

One day in his rookie season of 1915, the manager of the Browns, Branch Rickey, who had once been Sisler's college baseball coach, said to him: "George, I know you can pitch, and become famous as a big-league hurler. But what my team now needs most of all is a good first baseman. I want you to play first base."

George Sisler accepted his new assignment most reluctantly, but so versatile and magnificent were his skills as a complete ballplayer that he soon was in a class by himself as a first baseman. Before long, he was hailed far and wide as not only the most graceful first baseman ever seen but the equal of any first baseman in history. They nicknamed him Gorgeous George. His grace, ability and technique were matchless. He was the nearest thing to the perfect ballplayer, for he could do everything — field, hit, throw and run. Moreover, his smartness on a ball field was unexcelled.

Gorgeous George matched his magnificent fielding with phenomenal hitting. A picture player at first base, he made the most impossible plays look easy. By his third season in the majors, he was more than just a .300-plus hitter. His batting averages rose to .353, .341, .352, .371, .407 and .420. So phenomenal was his hitting that in his first eight seasons in the majors he compiled a batting average of .367.

In the 1920 season, when Gorgeous George zoomed to a .420 batting average, he slashed out 257 safe hits — the most hits ever made by a major-league player in a single season.

Once in a single season he batted safely in forty-one consecutive games. He also was one of baseball's greatest bunters and as an unusual base runner he averaged a stolen base nearly every three games.

At the height of his fame as baseball's greatest and most graceful first baseman, fate stopped George Sisler's career. He was only twenty-nine when he was stricken with acute sinusitis which affected his optic nerves and left him with double vision. He was out of baseball the entire year of 1923 while doctors tried to save him from a creeping blindness.

George Sisler fought a grim and courageous battle to retain his eyesight and resume his playing in the major leagues. He won that battle and he returned to the majors but he was no longer the fantastic first baseman that he had been before his eye trouble.

Nevertheless, upon his return to the big leagues, and despite his weakened eyesight, Gorgeous George continued to star as an outstanding first baseman for eight more seasons. Surprisingly, he had three more 200-hit seasons and twice he batted better than .340.

In his sixteen years in the major leagues he had played in 2,055 games, collected 2,812 hits, and left behind him a lifetime batting average of .341.

Now, the once fabulous first baseman George Sisler dwells in baseball's Hall of Fame. He was the man who was perhaps the nearest thing to a perfect ballplayer ever to be seen in the major leagues.

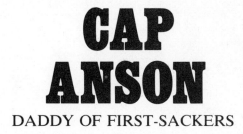

CAP ANSON

DADDY OF FIRST-SACKERS

BORN: Adrian Constantine Anson
     April 17, 1852, Marshalltown, Iowa
DIED: April 14, 1922, Chicago, Illinois
HEIGHT: 6'1"   WEIGHT: 220 lbs.
Threw and batted right-handed
Lifetime average (27 years): .339

Cap Anson was in a class by himself among the early great stars of big-league baseball. No man ever starred in big-league baseball for as many years as he did. His active career spanned three generations of ballplayers. He was the connecting link between old and modern major-league baseball. He starred for twenty-seven years.

A baseball pro at nineteen, after dropping out of Notre Dame University, Adrian Anson became the first great first baseman in history. Because of his matchless playing and his tremendous influence on the game, he is regarded to this day as the "daddy" of all great first basemen.

An incomparable guardian of first base, with matchless fielding skills, he was also one of the greatest hitters in the history of baseball. As a batsman, his slugging struck terror in the hearts of big-league pitchers for almost three decades. For twenty-four seasons he always batted over .300 and he was the first in history to hit .400 twice, with .407 and .421. He also was the first big-league player in history to reach the 3,000-hit class. His lifetime total was 3,081 safe hits. Five times he won the National League batting championship, and he wound up with a lifetime batting average of .339. They called him

Cap because Anson was everything a real captain is supposed to be. At the height of his fabulous career, Cap Anson was more than a national baseball hero. His name was synonymous with baseball. For he was a ballplayer of integrity, sobriety, personal purity and dignity.

He came to the Chicago club of the National League in 1876 as an accomplished first baseman, second baseman, third baseman, and catcher too, and he remained with that team for twenty-two seasons. Only three years after coming to the Chicago club, he became the playing manager of that team. He became the greatest playing manager in the history of big-league baseball. Cap Anson piloted Chicago to fifteen first-division finishes and five pennants in his nineteen years as a playing manager. When he finally left the Chicago club at age forty-five, that team was long known thereafter as the Orphans.

It was Cap Anson, the foremost baseball strategist of his time, who originated the hit-and-run play in major-league competition. As a playing manager, the daddy of all great first basemen was a fanatical stickler for rigid physical conditioning for himself as well as his players. He hounded them to keep trim and fit, watch their diets, and keep regular sleeping hours. He was an inspiring example of the good life for all ballplayers. Playing in an era when most ballplayers were tough and rough, powerful Cap Anson at times used his fists as well as his sharp tongue to discipline his players who broke training rules. But while most of his players feared him, all respected and loved him.

The start of each baseball season was always a trying time for Cap Anson. For invariably his players would report for action, hog-fat and woefully out of condition after a winter of loafing or high living. But in 1886, the fabulous first baseman Cap Anson decided to do something radically novel in big-league history to help his team-mates. Several weeks before the start of that baseball season, he ordered all of his Chicago players to report for duty. When the puzzled players showed up, Cap Anson took them to a training camp he had set up in Hot Springs, Arkansas. There, he put his players through daily rigorous training sessions to whip them into good physical playing shape for the coming baseball season. Although most of the players grumbled and complained, nevertheless, when that year's baseball campaign began, the Chicago players were in such fine physical playing condition that they breezed to a National League pennant.

When the other baseball managers saw what player-manager Cap Anson had accomplished with his pre-season innovation, they soon also made use of his "crazy invention" by setting up pre-season training camps of their own for their respective teams. Thus started "spring training" for all major-league players.

In 1897, when Cap Anson completed his twenty-second season for the Chicago team as baseball's greatest first baseman, while still hitting over .300 though he was forty-five years old, so great was his popularity with the baseball fans that a fund of $50,000 was raised by public subscription as a farewell gift for him. But with magnificent pride Cap Anson refused to accept the money from his worshipping admirers with the explanation that pro baseball owed him nothing for his glorious twenty-seven years in the game.

The incomparable Cap Anson retained his awesome fame and popularity as a baseball idol long after his departure from this world. In 1939 he was admitted to baseball's Hall of Fame to be remembered as one of the game's greatest men.

If in time it should be forgotten that he was a fantastic ballplayer, a matchless big-league manager, and an outstanding pacemaker, what Cap Anson originated for the good of the national pastime will never be forgotten. For he was the inventor of spring training.

JACKIE ROBINSON

HE SHATTERED A BARRIER

BORN: Jack Roosevelt Robinson
   January 31, 1919, Cairo, Georgia
DIED: October 24, 1972, Stamford, Connecticut
HEIGHT: 6′   WEIGHT: 215 lbs.
Threw and batted right-handed
Lifetime batting average (10 years): .311

I t may be hard for young baseball fans to believe there was ever a time — a very long time — when no black man could ever play in the big leagues. But in fact it was not until 1947 that Jackie Robinson became the first member of his race to play in the major leagues, and he broke the color barrier in America's national pastime forever. He was indeed the symbol of the black revolution in baseball. That story is now legend.

No baseball hero ever emerged from more humble, impoverished and less promising beginnings than Jackie Robinson. He was born into a family of sharecroppers on a shabby cotton plantation in Georgia, the grandson of a slave. He grew up in California, where his boyhood was hard. His father had wandered off to parts unknown, leaving behind his deserted wife with a brood of five hungry children. To survive, Jackie's mother toiled as a domestic and washwoman. Young Jackie did odd jobs after school, shining shoes, running errands and delivering newspapers.

It was in high school that he first attracted attention as an unusual

athlete, excelling in football, baseball, basketball and track. His versatility earned him an athletic scholarship to college. He was however reluctant to accept it because he wanted to work to ease his mother's burden. But she insisted that he accept his opportunity for a college education.

"It's your only chance to become a somebody in this world," she told him.

He wound up at the University of California at Los Angeles where he gained fame as one of America's finest all-around athletes. He was an All-American in football, an outstanding star in baseball, basketball and track, and a top boxer too.

When World War II broke out, Jackie Robinson enlisted in the United States Army as a private, but rose to the rank of an officer.

Upon the war's end, when he was mustered out of service, Jackie found himself broke and jobless. He turned to professional baseball for a livelihood. He accepted an offer to play for a well-known Negro barnstorming baseball team, the Kansas City Monarchs, for a salary of $400 a month.

That was where Branch Rickey, a part owner and general manager of the Brooklyn Dodgers (now of Los Angeles), discovered Jackie Robinson. A onetime major-league manager, Branch Rickey had become a shrewd, bold, ingenious, and visionary baseball executive who nursed a secret plan to revolutionize organized baseball. In Jackie Robinson, he saw that special player he needed for his great and noble experiment.

One day, a puzzled Jackie Robinson was ushered into Branch Rickey's private office for a secret meeting behind locked doors.

"Jackie, I know you can play ball as well as anyone now in the major leagues," said Branch Rickey. "But what I want to know is if you have the guts and courage to help me break baseball's color barrier that's been a part of the game ever since big-league baseball began."

"Do you want a ballplayer who isn't afraid to fight?" asked Robinson.

"I want a special man with courage enough to play in the majors and not fight back with his fists," said Rickey.

He then outlined what was in store for Jackie Robinson if he dared challenge the unwritten exclusionary rule of organized baseball and told him about all the hostility, cruel abuse and ostracism he would have to endure as the first black player in the major leagues.

"They'll call you a lousy nigger wherever you play. They'll try to hurt you, throw pitches at your head, cut you with their spikes, curse and abuse you at every turn, to make you fight. What will you do then, Jackie?" the boss of the Brooklyn Dodgers screamed into Robinson's face.

"Mr. Rickey, if you want me to play in the big leagues, then I'm not afraid to try it, and I'll play ball, by your rules," said Jackie Robinson.

The veteran baseball man nodded his wise head and a warm smile lit up his face for he knew that his search was over. In Jackie Robinson he had found that very special fearless, courageous, intelligent and skillful black ballplayer to blaze a new trail in major-league baseball and chart the path for many others in years to come.

Jackie Robinson was twenty-eight years old in 1947 when he first put on a major-league uniform to play in the big leagues. In the beginning, he had to endure brutalities and humiliations never known by any other rookie in history. He took merciless riding and racial taunts from rival players and fans. Bigots threatened him with physical injury and even his life was threatened if he continued to play in the majors.

Rival players threatened to strike rather than play against him if he remained in the Dodgers' lineup and even some of his own teammates refused to play on the same team with a black man. He couldn't live in the same hotels or eat in the same restaurants as his teammates.

It was a brutal ordeal in the beginning. But Jackie Robinson in silent dignity endured it all without any retaliation. He stoically and courageously battled his way to recognition and renown as a major-league player. From his rookie season, he revealed himself as one of the most exciting and competitive players in history. A natural firebrand, he carried a flaming spirit into every game he played. Often, singlehandedly he could turn a game around. He aroused fear with his bat, created havoc on the base paths, and in the field he was electrifying. He was so outstanding in his freshman year in the majors, that he was named Rookie of the Year and he helped the Dodgers win the National League pennant.

As the seasons passed, with his dynamic and matchless skills as a first, second or third baseman and outfielder, he forced the hostile baseball world to accept him as a genuine major-league star. He excelled at whatever position he played for his team. He took risks shunned by other performers and he always was at his best when it counted the most. Big-league managers often commented in awe that there never was another player in the majors who could beat you in as many different ways as Jackie Robinson.

In 1949 he posted one of the finest individual records ever. He played in 156 games, led all second basemen in double plays, again led his league in stolen bases, made 203 hits, drove in 124 runs, scored 122 times, and his .342 batting average was the highest in the majors that season. He climaxed that glorious year with another "first" in baseball history, being voted the Most Valuable Player of the National League — the first black ever to be so honored. He was chosen six times for the National League All-Star team.

In the ten years he starred for the Brooklyn Dodgers, Jackie Robinson sparked and inspired them to six pennants.

In 1957, at the age of thirty-eight, although he was still a much-wanted and very highly paid player, Jackie Robinson, the baseball pioneer, decided that he had had enough of big-league glories. He retired from the game and went on to glory in many other areas of American life. He left behind him a magnificent ten-year record of major-league greatness — 1,518 hits, more than 200 stolen bases, a .311 lifetime batting average, a flock of World Series records, and the admiration and respect of the entire baseball world as one of the greatest players of major-league history.

In 1962, as soon as he became eligible to have baseball's greatest honor bestowed upon him, Jackie Robinson again made history by being elected to the Hall of Fame — the first black man to be so honored.

His fame as a baseball pioneer, in the finest sense of the word, never faded. Even twenty-five years after he first played in the majors, the baseball world was still bestowing honors upon him. He lived long enough to see blacks and other minorities comprise nearly half of all the players in the two major leagues, with many of them ranking among the greatest stars in history.

On October 24, 1972, when Jackie Robinson suddenly died at the age of fifty-three, not only a shocked baseball world grieved for him, but an entire nation as well mourned the passing of this truly great American. The president of the United States expressed the country's love and admiration of Jackie Robinson best when he said in a farewell to him:

"His courage, his sense of brotherhood, and his brilliance on the playing field brought a new human dimension not only to the game of baseball but to every area of American life where black and white people work side by side. This nation to which he gave so much in his lifetime will miss Jackie Robinson, but his example will continue to inspire us for years to come."

ROGERS HORNSBY

A RAJAH WITH A BAT

BORN: Rogers Hornsby
       April 27, 1896, Winters, Texas
DIED: January 5, 1963, Chicago, Illinois
HEIGHT: 5'11½"   WEIGHT: 200 lbs.
Threw and batted right-handed
Lifetime batting average (23 years): .358

Rogers Hornsby, whose status as the greatest right-handed hitter of all time is seldom challenged and who sailed into the Hall of Fame without argument, had another attribute which is not often recalled: his excellent running speed. In his time, he outran the dash men on the track teams of two great universities and even in his latter years he could outspeed the fastest rookies.

But it was his hitting which made the Rajah famous, for he was batting form personified. As proof, he won the batting title of the National League six times in a row, seven times in all. And during one five-year span (1921–1925), he gave the most incredible and devastating performance ever achieved by a major leaguer.

Over that period the Rajah won five batting titles in succession, and hit more than .400 three times. Also during that fantastic period of slugging greatness, he went to bat 2,679 times and he hit safely 1,078 times, averaging 216 hits a season and an overall batting average of .402. No player in history ever matched that unbelievable hitting record.

It didn't appear that a batter of such magnitude was being born when Rogers Hornsby first appeared at a St. Louis Cardinal clubhouse late in the season of 1915. He was a bush leaguer out of Winters, Texas, fresh from the Western Association, and he was a strange one. Nineteen years old with rosy cheeks, he stretched to five feet, eleven and a half inches, but weighed barely 130 lbs. A bat was so heavy in his hands that he had to choke up on the handle. He was a mediocre infielder and he looked hopeless at bat. He was so unimpressive a player that when the club owner saw him he objected to paying the rookie the promised salary of ninety dollars a month. Instead, he was offered sixty a month to play for the Cardinals.

But Hornsby, even at nineteen, was keen, intelligent and quick to learn, and he was zealously determined to play big-league ball. He got into eighteen games and made fourteen hits before that season ended.

Advised by a kindly manager to fatten up if he wanted to continue playing for the Cardinals, Hornsby spent the first winter after he broke in on his uncle's farm consuming gargantuan quantities of steaks, milk, cheese, potatoes and ice cream and sleeping twelve hours a night.

The following spring when he reported back to the Cardinals, he not only had fattened up to 165 lbs. but was also strong enough to swing a bat by gripping it at the end of the handle. The change in his batting form was immediately apparent, for in the 139 games he played that season, he belted out 155 hits for a .313 batting average.

Hornsby was playing second, third and shortstop in those days, but soon he was an established second baseman, perhaps the best baseball ever saw. He was sure-handed and had a strong accurate arm and on double plays he dared the base runner to dump him. Often he would let the runner have it between the eyes, discouraging further interference.

No player was ever more dedicated to the game of baseball and its glories than the serious-minded Rajah. Baseball was his way of life. During his long playing career (1915–1937), Hornsby never smoked, drank or frolicked as most big-league players did. He wouldn't even go to the movies for he felt that seeing the "flicks" would strain his keen eyesight. He was a "loner" on the glory road to big-league fame and fortune.

His discipline paid off. He became a hitter without a weakness. No matter what opposing pitchers tried to do in stopping him, he was prepared. In 1924, his greatest season, he played in 143 games and made 227 hits, including 43 doubles, 14 triples and 25 homers, to conclude a year with a .424 batting average — the highest in modern major-league history.

Hornsby was the only player in National League history to bat .400 or better three times. Seven times he paced the league in total bases. He became the first player in history to win the majors triple crown (batting average, home runs, runs-batted-in, for a single season) more than once.

In twenty-three years and 2,259 big-league games, he made 2,930 hits, slugged 302 home runs, collected 1,579 runs and compiled a dazzling lifetime batting average of .358 — a mark surpassed only by the immortal left-handed batting wizard, Ty Cobb.

Despite his glamorous hitting marks, Hornsby was something less than a matinee idol. He had a blunt personality which alienated his teammates, his employers, other ballplayers and often the fans. Because the Rajah's tongue was as sharp as his spikes, he had a checkered career. He played for five different major-league clubs. But he was so valuable a second baseman that once one club had to pay more than $200,000 to purchase him from another club.

Later he was to become a manager, though he had little patience with young players who did not have his devotion and ability. Still he led the St. Louis Cardinals to their first pennant and world championship and the Chicago Cubs to a National League pennant.

On January 5, 1963, at the age of sixty-six, the fiery Rogers Hornsby succumbed to his only weakness — a failing heart. But he departed from this world unique in his glory as a Hall of Fame baseball hero — ever to be regarded as the greatest right-handed hitter in the game's history.

NAPOLEON LAJOIE

THE GRACEFUL FRENCHMAN

BORN: Napoleon Lajoie
   September 5, 1875, Woonsocket, Rhode Island
DIED: February 7, 1959, Daytona Beach, Florida
HEIGHT: 6'1"   WEIGHT: 195 lbs.
Threw and batted right-handed
Lifetime average (21 years): .339

In the Hall of Fame, the only immortal especially noted for his elegance of movement at bat and afield is Napoleon Lajoie. Not only was the legendary Frenchman one of the foremost second basemen in history, but he also was the most graceful player who ever performed in big-league baseball.

When Lajoie was still a boy, he was already doing a man's work to help support his widowed mother and her brood of seven children. He worked in a cotton mill. Only on Sundays could he find time to play some sandlot baseball. As he grew older, he drove a hack for a livery stable through the streets of Woonsocket, Rhode Island.

However, because of his unusual sandlot baseball playing, he was plucked out of obscurity and turned into a professional ballplayer. In 1896, the Fall River club of the old New England League hired him as a second baseman for one hundred dollars a month. When the 21-year-old Frenchman learned how much money he would be paid to play pro ball, he gleefully exclaimed: "By Gar! From now on, Napoleon will play only baseball!"

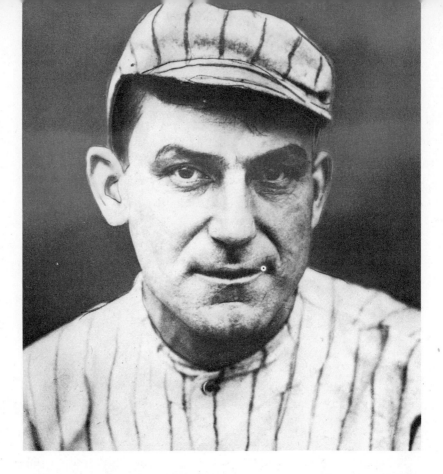

And how he played it! He was phenomenal from the beginning. In his pro debut he hit .429 to win the New England League batting title and immediate promotion to the big leagues. The Philadelphia Phillies bought him for $1,500. He remained in the major leagues for twenty-one active years, and no other keystone guardian in major-league history ever topped his skills as a fielder and batter, nor his incomparable smoothness and grace on a diamond. Every move of his on a ball field was "poetry in motion." With astonishing nonchalance he made the most difficult fielding plays look so ridiculously simple that often baseball fans had the impression that he wasn't trying. He scooped up the hardest infield drives with unbelievable assurance and ease.

At the plate, his right-handed swing was so smooth and so accurate that all rival pitchers came to believe that he had no batting weakness. He hit pitches to all fields, and for distance. His bunting was matchless.

In 1901, when the National League Philadelphia club refused to raise Lajoie's season's salary to $2,500, he jumped to the newly organized American League to play for the Philadelphia Athletics. In the very first season he played in that infant major league, Napoleon Lajoie set such a blistering hitting pace that it hasn't been matched by any American League player to this day. He played in 131 games, appeared 543 times at bat, and went hitless in only 17 of them, winding up with 229 hits, to set the all-time American League batting mark of .422, for a single season. It was the first of his three batting championships. For sixteen years he proceeded to top the .300 mark.

However, the big graceful Frenchman played for the Philadelphia Athletics only one season because the owner of the Phillies club obtained a court injunction preventing him from playing in the city of Philadelphia. So, to restore peace and harmony in that controversy between the National and American League for Napoleon Lajoie's matchless services as a ballplayer, he was traded to the Cleveland club.

In the following twelve years he starred for the Cleveland ball club. So phenomenal and sensational were his diamond exploits that the team became widely known as his. The team became known everywhere as the Cleveland Naps, so nicknamed in his honor. For five seasons Napoleon Lajoie was also their playing manager.

Lajoie played his final game in the major leagues when he was past forty-one. His final hit was a booming triple. It completed his 2,475th big-league game. His legacy to baseball history was 3,251 safe hits, 1,503 runs, 396 stolen bases, and a lifetime batting average of .339. Also, several records exist as testimony of his keystone fielding greatness.

His fabulous fame as the most graceful baseball player ever seen never faded. When Napoleon Lajoie was sixty years old, the major leagues lured him out of retirement to star in an educational motion picture demonstrating the proper and graceful form at bat and afield.

Although fate had denied this phenomenal second baseman the glory of playing even once with a pennant-winning team, nevertheless, there was no question when the Hall of Fame came into being, that Napoleon Lajoie would be one of its original honored members. He was sixty-two when he saw himself officially identified in the Cooperstown shrine as the most graceful diamond immortal who ever played in the major leagues.

PIE
TRAYNOR

HE COOLED THE HOT CORNER

BORN: Harold Joseph Traynor
November 11, 1899, Framingham, Massachusetts
DIED: March 16, 1972, Pittsburgh, Pennsylvania
HEIGHT: 6'1½"   WEIGHT: 175 lbs.
Threw and batted right-handed
Lifetime batting average (17 years): .320

When Pie Traynor was inevitably inducted into the Hall of Fame in 1948, it was generally conceded that the Hall had installed the premier third baseman of all time. Old timers recalled a joke that was prevalent in National League press boxes when Pie was in his Pittsburgh Pirate heyday. In describing a play that had just happened, the writers would chorus: "Joe Doakes doubled over the third-base bag — and Pie Traynor threw him out at first base."

That is how superbly Traynor played his position. He was as close to perfection as any third baseman has ever been. In the seventeen seasons he played for Pittsburgh, he set the standard for ultimate third-base skill. For he had a great arm, great hands, great body control, quickness and speed, and a fine disposition. He was an ideal team man — and he could run with speed.

He was born into a family with no sports background, the son of a printer. But his father encouraged him to take part in sports, and young Harold developed into a fine baseball, football and hockey player. But as he grew older, baseball, his first love, crowded out the other sports and he lived just to perform on the diamond.

In boyhood he came to be known as "Pie" because of his outstanding skill in local ball games. Whenever he played with the older and bigger boys on the playground of a parochial school, and his team won, the neighborhood priest who also acted as umpire invariably would reward the triumphant players with treats of their choosing. After each winning game, young Harold, upon being asked what he wanted, would say: "I'll have a piece of pie, Father." Thus he acquired the nickname that became his trademark for the rest of his days.

Even before he was fifteen years old, Pie managed to perform on a big-league diamond along with major leaguers. This was accomplished by his sneaking into Fenway Park in Boston one day. Then, sitting in the grandstand with his baseball glove, he noticed that the Red Sox third baseman had left his position for a few minutes during infield practice. Pie raced onto the field and began scooping up grounders at third, and managed to get in quite a few plays with the rest of the Red Sox infield before the manager spotted him and angrily chased him off the field.

A few years later, Traynor was thrown out of another big-league park. He tried out with the Boston Braves, but the manager took one look at Pie, who was lanky and skinny at over six feet, and told him to go home and forget about a baseball career.

But three years later, at age twenty, Pie Traynor was in the big leagues, and he was to stay there for seventeen years as a player and six more as a manager. He was a shortstop in the beginning, but almost immediately he found a niche at third base.

Despite his rangy build, Traynor began to astonish the baseball world with electrifying performances at the hot corner of the infield. He conceded hitters nothing. He flashed the quickest hands anybody could remember seeing, and daily he made incredible fielding plays on any ball hit in his direction. With supreme grace, with gloved or bare hand, he speared the hardest-hit line drives over the bag or to his left, plucked fouls out of the stands, scooted to short left field to snare pop flies, scooped up bunts on the run, and followed with superb rifle throws to first with the most powerful throwing arm ever seen on a third baseman.

Traynor coupled his superb fielding with a hot and consistent bat. One season he blasted out 208 hits, including nineteen triples, for a .338 average, and subsequently he posted averages of .342, .356 and .366. In his seventeen years in the majors, over a span of 1,941 games and 7,558 appearances at the plate, he made 2,416 safe hits, more than any other third baseman in history. He posted a lifetime average of .320 — highest of all third basemen now in the Hall of Fame.

Pie also was the first third sacker to play in as many as 1,941 major-league games, and even today holds the National League record for most putouts by a third baseman in a career, 2,288. His range in the field was attested to by the times he led his league in putouts (seven) and assists (three), and he was the only player at his position ever to make more than 300 assists three times. His matchless play at third base sparked the Pirates to their very first World Series championship.

Throughout his long career, Traynor won the respect of everybody connected with the game. He was a soft-spoken gentleman, who never raised his voice to teammates, rival players, or even umpires. He maintained his modest and polite demeanor despite the acclaim which rightfully fell on him as the supreme third baseman. Teammates always said that he never lost his temper and refrained from profanity at all times, no matter what the provocation.

Pie's legendary career came to a sudden end when he was only thirty-four and still performing dazzling feats at third base. One day during a tight game, he slid into home plate for a run that helped his Pirates win another game. But on that ninth-inning play, the rival catcher landed heavily with both knees on Traynor's extended right arm. Pie's mighty throwing arm was never the same again.

Pittsburgh refused to let him go, however, and he was hired as player-manager. Curiously, his first major decision as a Pirate pilot was to bench himself as a regular third baseman. After six years as a manager, he quietly gave up the job to become a Pirate scout.

When he was elected to the Hall of Fame in 1948, he was still the same quiet-mannered, gentlemanly figure he had always been. He accepted the accolades modestly.

This did not surprise his friends and former teammates, for that was the way he had lived his glamorous time in the major leagues. They added a postscript. They said that Pie Traynor set a standard for playing third base in the big leagues that will always be used as the ultimate measure in hot-corner skill.

For all baseball time, the name of Pie Traynor will remain synonymous with third base.

WALTER MARANVILLE

THE MISCHIEVOUS RABBIT

BORN: James Walter Vincent Maranville,
   November 11, 1891, Springfield, Massachusetts
DIED: January 5, 1954, New York, New York
HEIGHT: 5'5"   WEIGHT: 155 lbs.
Threw and batted right-handed
Lifetime batting average (23 years): .258

C alled the Rabbit, he was one of the smallest men ever to play in the big leagues, for he stood only sixty-five inches tall and barely weighed 155 lbs. soaking wet. But despite his tiny stature, he starred in the major leagues for twenty-three years and played in 2,670 games. He carved a niche for himself in baseball history as as great a shortstop as ever played the game.

But little Walter Maranville was more than a fabulous shortstop. He was also one of the best liked, most amusing, and one of the funniest players baseball ever had. He was a colorful, rollicking, clowning, mischief-making imp who spread laughter wherever he went.

The Rabbit was not only a glove magician in the short field, but was also a tremendous clutch performer. At the shortshop position, he covered more ground than players twice his size. He made the most impossible plays look easy. His "basket catch" became his trademark. Possessed with the smallest hands in baseball, he always caught a ball with both hands held high against his body. His

vest-pocket catch seemed like a comedy stunt just to make baseball fans laugh.

He came to the major leagues to play for the Boston Braves before he was twenty-one years old. He continued playing in the majors until he was forty-four. A blithe spirit, the spunky, lionhearted and aggressive Rabbit feared no one when he was scampering about on a ballfield. Whenever he guarded the base paths, he defied baseball's biggest and roughest bullies. Blocking all base runners who came his way, the Rabbit would often not only tag out a runner sliding into second, but climax the putout by sitting triumphantly on top of the embarrassed base runner.

When the Rabbit was only in his third major-league season, he became linked with one of baseball's greatest miracles. He sparked a Boston Braves team floundering in last place late in the 1914 season to start a miraculous surge to glory which continued until that surprising Boston team had won the National League pennant and swept the World Series in four straight games to become baseball champions of the world. In that memorable season of baseball's miraculous triumph, the matchless Rabbit played in 156 games, accepted a record number of chances by handling 1,046 balls, made 407 putouts, and 574 assists.

Season after season, the amazing Rabbit led the National League in fielding, and even when he had reached forty, he was still spry enough to lead all major-league shortstops of his time in fielding. Though not a great batter at the plate, tiny Maranville was still a fearless and timely hitter, great enough to collect 2,605 safe hits in his major-league career.

A gay blade ever in search of fun and laughs, that impish shrimp was unique as a mischief-maker. Many of his antics and capers on and off the field were unbelievable. He was always doing something surprising and amusing. Sometimes he crawled between an umpire's legs to get to the plate. Often he appeared in public places with a pet parrot or monkey perched on his shoulder. He kept pigeons in the closets of his hotel room and live fish often swam in his bathtub. At times, a flock of rabbits scampered over the furniture of his hotel room.

Once, he waded into the fountain of a hotel lobby just to catch a goldfish and take a bite out of it. Another time, for a lark and to frighten his teammates, he climbed out on the narrow ledge of his hotel-room window — twelve floors above the ground. On still another occasion, when the Rabbit was on the way to the ball park, he suddenly jumped, fully clothed, into a river and swam across a long stretch of water rather than ride across the bridge spanning the river.

Wherever the clowning Rabbit played (and he starred for five major-league teams in his time) he indulged in his hilarious tomfoolery, and no man ever had more fun playing in the big leagues than tiny Walter Maranville. In 1925, even when he became the player-manager of the Chicago Cubs, he still continued as a happy little clown on the hunt for laughs. He was that team's leader for every practical joke and every wild escapade.

The puckish Rabbit remained a carefree boy all through his big-league career until suddenly it came to a dramatic finish when he was forty-four years old. He was playing in a spring-training exhibition game when the aged Rabbit tried to steal home with the winning run of that game. But a husky young catcher half his age blocked the plate on that play and tiny Maranville crashed into him, and wound up in the dust with a broken leg. Though he was in extreme pain, the spunky Rabbit yelled at the umpire: "I was safe! He never tagged me! Look where my foot is to score the run."

Sure enough, Maranville's broken leg rested limply at the edge of home plate. When he was carried off the field, he told his down-hearted teammates: "Well, guys, this old man had to stop playing sometime. Maybe this is the quickest and best way to go out of the majors!"

He never again played in the major leagues.

Indeed, that incredible clowning Rabbit carved a man-sized niche for himself in baseball history. In 1954, baseball's most coveted and greatest honor was bestowed upon him in tribute to his greatness as a big-league shortstop. He was elected to the Hall of Fame, to be forever remembered.

Ironically, little Walter Maranville just missed tasting the joy of his final and greatest moment of baseball glory, for only days before his enshrinement at Cooperstown he died.

LUKE APPLING

MAN WITH ACHES AND PAINS

BORN: Lucius Benjamin Appling
    April 2, 1909, High Point, North Carolina
HEIGHT: 5'11"   WEIGHT: 200 lbs.
Threw and batted right-handed
Lifetime batting average (20 years): .310

The most imaginative and most durable hypochondriac ever to win fame in the major leagues was shortstop Luke Appling, who starred for the Chicago White Sox longer than any other short-stop in history. No player in big-league annals ever had such a quixotic attitude toward his health as did Luke Appling. His constant and ceaseless concern with all the real and imaginary ailments afflict-ing his anatomy earned him a unique nickname in baseball history — Ol' Aches and Pains. It was a miracle he survived as a player in the majors for as long as he did — twenty-one seasons.

Never a baseball day passed without Luke Appling worrying and groaning about his ailments. Often he would show up for games complaining of suffering with weak legs, an injured back, a sore arm, double vision, or other physical troubles. But somehow he always suited up, dragged himself onto the field, and gave a spectacular performance at shortstop. He had few equals in history when it came to glove brilliance. Whenever he complained most of his ill health it was a cinch that on that day he would make the key plays and collect several base knocks.

He was one of the game's toughest clutch hitters who placed his hits to all fields. A clever bat manipulator, he was an amazing bunter. Owner of an uncanny eye, his matchless ability to foul off pitches he didn't like became his trademark at the plate. It was not unusual for Luke Appling to foul off as many as a dozen pitches at a time, much to the dismay and annoyance of rival hurlers.

In 1936, he reached his peak as a constant .300-plus hitter when he became the first and only shortstop in history to lead the American League in batting. That season, he won the crown with a .388 batting mark. Seven years later, he again won the league batting championship.

The most durable of all shortstops in major-league history, Ol' Aches and Pains played more games in the short field than any other shortstop in big-league annals. During his twenty-one consecutive years with the Chicago White Sox, he played at shortstop in 2,218 games — the all-time record. He led shortstops in assists for seven seasons, 7,220 for another major-league mark. He set American League records for lifetime putouts too, with 4,349. He collected a lifetime total of 2,749 hits and wound up with a .310 lifetime batting average.

Ol' Aches and Pains, despite all his constant complaints of ill health, never played less than 100 games each season. Most of the time his manager took his complaints with a grain of salt. Even when he was the unhappy victim of a real injury, it was difficult for him to convince others of his misfortune.

Once during an important game, Ol' Aches and Pains attempted a daring steal of second, and he beat the throw to the base with a spectacular slide. But when the dust cleared, Luke Appling was lying writhing on the ground, moaning that his leg was broken. No one believed him and everybody chuckled.

"Get up, you faker!" snapped his manager. "You can't con me into giving you the rest of the afternoon off!"

"Appling! You're cluttering up the infield," said the amused umpire. "Get up and let's play ball."

But this time, Luke Appling really had a broken leg and it put him out of action for part of that season.

It was while playing for Oglethorpe University that Luke Appling first attracted the attention of big-league baseball scouts. He was twenty-one when he came to the Chicago White Sox and was to remain a star for that team for an unprecedented twenty-one years. When past forty-one, he was still outrunning, outhitting, and out-hustling major-league youngsters who were not even born when he first broke into organized baseball.

The "mostest shortstop" in major-league history finally quit playing in the big league at the end of the 1950 season. However, he had to wait fourteen years before he officially entered the Hall of Fame. When it happened, the fabled Luke Appling said: "It's the greatest and happiest day of my life! I've had other honors in baseball, but nothing like this. But gee, I wish I wasn't aching so much today!"

It was typical of the legendary Ol' Aches and Pains to feel that way on the biggest baseball day of his life.

HONUS WAGNER

A FLYING DUTCHMAN

BORN: John Peter Wagner
    February 24, 1874, Carnegie, Pennsylvania
DIED: December 6, 1955, Carnegie, Pennsylvania
HEIGHT: 5'11"   WEIGHT: 200 lbs.
Threw and batted right-handed
Lifetime batting average (21 years): .329

When the gates of the Hall of Fame swung open for the first time in 1936, among the first to enter was the famed shortstop, John Peter (Honus) Wagner. There were many old-time observers who said that Hans was the greatest player of all time. On the Cooperstown plaque it says simply: "The Greatest Shortstop in Baseball History."

He was the son of a German immigrant and long before he saw a baseball he already had known life's hardships. At the age of twelve, he toiled in a Pennsylvania mine, loading coal cars. By eighteen, he had escaped from the dark pits to become a barber. However, by this time he had discovered baseball and he played it for amusement. It wasn't until he was twenty-one that he found the opportunity to start a professional baseball career. He got five dollars a week and board. The year was 1895.

He hardly looked like a ballplayer. He was powerfully built and had wide shoulders, but he was extremely awkward and ridiculously bowlegged. His gangling arms were unusually long and his huge hands looked like shovels.

75

His first few years as a pro player were neither easy nor happy. He was so unappreciated and so unwanted that one season he was forced to play for six different bush-league teams. Finally, in 1897, when he was past twenty-three, he crashed the big leagues to play for the munificent salary of $350 a month.

That year, his first in baseball, he batted .344 even though he didn't know which position he played best. He could perform at every position equally well, but eventually he settled down at shortstop. He was a strange and brilliant one. When he scooped up a grounder on a dusty field, the first fifteen feet in the fast flight of the ball was sometimes a dust cloud. One of his first basemen used to joke that he simply picked out the biggest object from the cloud to catch — and it was usually the ball.

His plays in the field bordered on the incredible. He made seemingly impossible plays, and he often threw runners out while sitting or lying on the turf. He caught, speared, ambushed and smothered everything within his tremendous reach, and he made 4,320 putouts and 5,664 assists while committing only 612 errors — a truly remarkable record. He never had an equal in starting or completing double plays.

As a hitter, the Flying Dutchman, as he was called, was a marvel to see. For seventeen years in the majors he batted .300 or better, including such glossy figures as .381 in 1900 and .363 in 1905. He played in 2,785 games, came to bat 10,427 times, hit safely 3,430 times and scored 1,740 runs. He is the only man in the long history of the National League who won the batting championship eight times.

Though bowlegged and seemingly clumsy, bearlike Hans had remarkable and deceptive speed as a base runner; only three other players in history surpassed him as a base stealer. His lifetime total was 720. No other player in the history of the National League ever matched the Flying Dutchman as a base burglar.

Honus Wagner had a simplistic view of life: baseball. His only two hobbies were tinkering with his automobile (one of the early ones) and giving boyish attention to his pets (of which he owned thirty-five at one time). He had few friends, none very close.

To play baseball was his passion. Nothing could tempt him away from the game. He did not like people making a fuss over his performances, however, and he spurned all offers to capitalize on his fame. Once, when he was the biggest hero of the National League, an offer came to appear on stage for $1,000 a week. His answer: "I'm no actor and no freak. I'm just a shortstop." And he turned it down.

He was so much in love with the game that when his playing days were over, he remained in the majors until 1951 as coach of the Pittsburgh club, on which he had had his glory days. Even later when he could no longer suit up, he took the trolley from his home in Carnegie, near Pittsburgh, to talk to young players about the game. His devotion to the game was unbounded, as was the devotion baseball fans held for him until his death in 1955, at the age of eighty-one.

In Pittsburgh, near the site where the greatest shortstop of all time made history for twenty-one years, there stands an eighteen-foot life-sized bronze statue. The inscription carved into it reads:

HONUS WAGNER: Erected by the fans of America, in honor of a baseball immortal, a champion of champions whose record on and off the playing field of the national game will ever stand as a monument to his own greatness and as an example and inspiration to the youth of our country.

CATCHERS
& PITCHERS

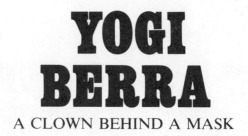

YOGI BERRA

A CLOWN BEHIND A MASK

BORN: Lawrence Peter Berra
May 12, 1925, St. Louis, Missouri
HEIGHT: 5'8"   WEIGHT: 191 lbs.
Threw right-handed and batted left-handed
Lifetime batting average (19 years): .285

When Yogi Berra, the squat, lovable little man who played in the majors for nineteen years, arrived in Cooperstown to be entered in the Hall of Fame in 1972, there were seven catchers who had made it before him. However, none of the others' credentials were as impressive as those chalked up by the New York Yankee receiver who began his playing days as something of a comic-strip character and a clown.

Berra, for instance, had played in the most games (2,120), had thrashed out the most hits (2,150), had scored the most runs (1,175) and had by far belted the most home runs (358) and driven in the most runs (1,430). Berra was also carrying a bushel basketful of World Series records, established in the fourteen postseason classics in which he participated — a record unparalleled in history.

It would be hard to imagine that all these honors were to befall Lawrence Peter Berra if one were to look at his early life and his rookie playing days. He was born on the Hill, the heavily populated Italian section of St. Louis, the son of an immigrant Italian bricklayer. All Yogi (he got the nickname from boyhood pals who said that

his odd appearance made him look like a yogi) wanted to do was play baseball. He was so impatient to get started that he didn't even finish grade school. At seventeen, he was catching in the minors for ninety dollars a month.

After spending two years in the service in World War II and half a season with the Yankees' top farm club in Newark, Berra was called up to the big club in 1946 — and he was to stay there for eighteen glorious seasons.

At the beginning it wasn't easy. His looks were against him, for one thing. He had a stubby build. He was thick-shouldered with hardly any neck and he had an ugly face. No big-league rookie ever looked less like a ballplayer than Yogi. He made blundering remarks and was childishly gullible. He was the target of all dugout humor, teased by his teammates as well as rival players. Everybody agreed that he looked something like an ape and played like a clown. Rival players taunted him mercilessly about his ugly looks and his ignorance.

But Berra took the cruel taunts with good humor. "What's the difference?" he used to say. "Maybe I ain't pretty, but I don't have to hit with my face."

Once his manager berated him for swinging at bad pitches, and said, "Yogi, when you're at bat I want you to think. Always think when you get up to hit."

"Gee, Skip," said Berra, grumbling, "how can a guy think and hit at the same time?"

Almost immediately Yogi swung a thunderous bat as a major leaguer. His catching left something to be desired, however. He misjudged foul pops, dropped balls, fell down chasing bunts and threw wildly to bases. Finally, the exasperated manager assigned Bill Dickey, the fabulous Hall of Famer once acclaimed the greatest of catchers, to work with Yogi in the hopes of making him a respectable major-league backstop.

Yogi told everybody about it. "Dickey is learnin' me his experiences," he said simply and joyously.

Soon the kinks were ironed out and Berra became not only a respectable catcher but a superior one. He called pitches excellently. His throwing improved. He was in charge in every game. As fans and players got to know him better, he won their affection, for he was always a gentle, kind and friendly human being. Yogi's naive sayings, his odd mannerisms and his funny verbal boners became treasured humor in baseball lore.

He became a brilliant ballplayer behind the plate as well as at bat. He is the only catcher in history to go through 148 consecutive major-league games without an error. He set the all-time record for most chances accepted by a catcher (9,493) and most putouts by a big-league backstop (8,696).

At bat, he was a terror. His 30 home runs in one year were the most ever hit by an American League catcher and five times he drove in more than 100 runs. He won the league's Most Valuable Player award three times, in 1951, 1954 and 1955. As a reward, he became the most highly paid catcher in major-league history in his time.

His worth to the New York Yankees was attested by the fact that in the eighteen years he played for them, the club won fourteen pennants and ten World Series championships.

It was in those postseason classics that Yogi's hard-nosed and magnificent approach paid off. With the chips down in the biggest and most important baseball event in sports, catcher Berra walked off with more World Series records than any other player in history, to establish himself as the most productive and greatest of all World Series heroes.

He played in more World Series games than anyone else in history (75). He was the first player in Series history to hit a pinch home run. He was at bat the most times (259), and he collected the most safe hits (71). He collected the most total bases (117). He made the most putouts (457) and most assists (36).

In 1963, his final season as a player, the countless fans who idolized the best fielding and hardest-hitting catcher the majors ever had staged a special day at the Yankee Stadium in Yogi Berra's honor. He was showered with money and expensive gifts as tributes to his greatness. On that occasion, the little gargoyle again revealed himself as a wonderful human being and a complete paradox.

The unlettered Kid from the Hill who as a boy had never even completed his formal education took all the money and the gifts which had been given him by his adoring fans and used them to set up a Yogi Berra Scholarship Fund which would supply financial aid for poor and ambitious youngsters wishing to acquire a college education.

In 1964, when the New York club elevated their beloved little catcher to manager of the Yankees, Yogi again surprised the baseball world with his leadership ability, and piloted his team to a pennant.

From beginning to end, the saga of Yogi Berra, the ugly duckling who became the greatest and richest catcher in the Hall of Fame, should inspire everyone to believe in baseball miracles.

ROY CAMPANELLA

THE HAPPIEST WARRIOR

BORN: Roy Campanella
        November 19, 1921, Philadelphia, Pennsylvania
HEIGHT: 5'9½"   WEIGHT: 205 lbs.
Threw and batted right-handed
Lifetime batting average (10 years): .276

Y ou have to be a man to be a big leaguer, but you have to have a lot of little boy in you, too!" So believed Roy Campanella all through his baseball career. He was both.

Born in the slums of Philadelphia, he was only fifteen when he began to play professional baseball. A team of grown men had offered him twenty-five dollars a week to be its catcher for weekend baseball games. However, Roy's mother, deeply religious, objected to her son's baseball playing on Sundays. To overcome her objections, young Roy played on Sundays only after he had gone to church and prayed. He was only sixteen when he left home to be a full-fledged professional baseball player. He became a baseball gypsy, barnstorming all over the United States, Canada, and South America, catching in ball games seven days a week, summer and winter. He caught more than 300 games a year, and earned almost three hundred dollars a month. So, Roy Campanella played pro baseball for almost twelve years, a wandering gypsy shining in the darkness of obscurity.

Finally came the most important and most glorious baseball day

84

of his life. He was twenty-seven when at long last he came to the major leagues to catch for the Brooklyn Dodgers. It was a historic day, for he was the first black catcher in big-league history.

It didn't take long for roly-poly Roy Campanella to establish himself as one of the brainiest catchers ever to squat behind a home plate in big-league competition. His skills as a magnificent fielder were astonishing. He was also a power hitter and a superb pitch handler. He was like a cat behind the plate, pouncing on bunts with amazing quickness, when rival batters placed them far in front of the plate. With a rifle arm he threw to bases with incredible accuracy. He was phenomenal in trapping and catching base stealers. In one season alone, he caught 138 out of 155 base burglars who had dared challenge his alertness and rifle arm. He was incomparable as a catcher for pickoffs of base runners. No tricky foul pop-ups hit behind the plate ever got away from quick and agile Campy, nicknamed the Cat.

Over the seasons, Roy Campanella established a number of major-league records for his ability as a backstop — for durability, most chances accepted, most putouts, and most no-hit games caught. He became one of the most feared slugging catchers in major-league history, as season after season, he stroked 30 or more homers. In 1953, he became the first backstop in big-league history to hit as many as 41 home runs in one season. He also became the first catcher in history to register as many as 142 runs-batted-in for one season. In all, he belted 242 home runs and collected 1,161 safe hits. Three times he was voted to be the Most Valuable Player of the National League.

But Roy Campanella, the majors' first black catcher, was more than a great backstop. A natural leader, he was indestructible as a catcher, surviving a startling assortment of injuries to achieve his stardom. Never was there a happier major-league ballplayer in history than the jolly Roy Campanella, who enjoyed a popularity second to none. He played every game with the ecstasy of a man in love with his work. For a decade he brought excitement and pleasure to millions of baseball fans, and though he became a baseball idol to youngsters and grown-ups all over America, he carried his fame with modesty and dignity. He was never too busy to talk to his fans, and went out of his way to help, advise and guide troubled youngsters. Wherever happy roly-poly Roy played, there was a sense of joy in the air.

So important and valuable a catcher was Roy Campanella to the Brooklyn Dodgers, that in the ten years he starred for them, he sparked them to five pennants.

He was only thirty-seven, and still one of baseball's most highly paid catchers when his dazzling major-league career suddenly came to an end. In January of 1958, baseball's happiest warrior was severely injured in an automobile mishap. Due to a medical miracle he survived that misfortune, which left him partially paralyzed and forced him to spend the rest of his life as a courageous invalid in a wheelchair.

However, in 1969, when crippled Roy Campanella was forty-seven, he again lived one happy and glorious day as a baseball great, for he saw himself enter the Hall of Fame at Cooperstown.

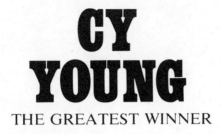

CY
YOUNG

THE GREATEST WINNER

BORN: Denton T. Young
        March 29, 1867, Gilmore, Ohio
DIED: November 4, 1955, Peoli, Ohio
HEIGHT: 6'2"   WEIGHT: 210 lbs.
Threw and batted right-handed
Lifetime pitching record (23 years):
        won 511, lost 313, .620

When the roll of pitching immortals was called at the Hall of Fame in Cooperstown, one man's record was so overwhelming that it bordered on the unbelievable. That record belonged to Denton Tecumseh (Cy) Young, who pitched for twenty-three consecutive years in the majors (a record which may never be broken) and won the astounding total of 511 games. In the history of the National and American Leagues, there have been fewer than 100 pitchers who've won 200 or more games in their own leagues. Cy Young won more than 200 in each of the leagues!

Born in the hills of Tuscarawas County in Ohio, Cy Young was twenty-two before he got into professional baseball. He came straight from a farm mowing machine to start throwing baseballs for forty dollars a month. He was the original country rube, tall (6 ft., 2 in.), sturdy (210 lbs.) and awkward. He wore a low-crowned derby hat and a shabby suit he had outgrown, sleeves failing to cover his wrists, trousers never reaching his ankles. He was truly a hick and he was an object of ridicule from all sides — until he began pitching.

Then the taunts stopped. At the beginning, the big hick had

nothing but blinding speed. Because he could pitch up a storm, he gained the appellation of Cyclone, later shortened to Cy. Though he was as wild as a March hare, he was practically unhittable.

He was in the minors only for a short time. After he had won five straight games and pitched a no-hitter with eighteen strikeouts, the Cleveland club bought his contract for $250 and a new suit of clothes.

In 1890, the big hayseed began pitching in the majors for seventy-five dollars a month and though he remained in the big leagues for twenty-three years, his salary never went above $5,000 a season. This didn't hinder him from almost immediately becoming the pitcher with the most wins ever. The season of 1892 he won thirty-six games and lost eleven for a stupendous .766 mark.

He had a rubber arm that never seemed to tire. In all, he pitched longer than any other starting hurler and participated in most games: 906. They encompassed 7,377 innings, light years ahead of any other pitcher before or since. He had 300 or more innings, sixteen times, and 200 or more innings nineteen times, those nineteen coming in succession.

Sixteen times Cy Young won twenty or more games in a season, fourteen of those in a row. In five seasons he won thirty or more games. He became the first pitcher in history to hurl three no-hit, no-run games, and the first of those, against Philadelphia in 1904, was a perfect game, twenty-seven hitters up, twenty-seven hitters down. It was the first no-hitter of the twentieth century.

He was the first man to pitch no-hitters in both major leagues. Once he extended a no-hit game into twenty-three consecutive hitless innings, a record which still stands almost seventy years later. His pitching cunning mowed down 2,819 batters on strikes, and despite his wildness as a youth, he ended his career with only 1,209 walks in 906 games, an average of 1.2 walks a game. One year he walked only twenty-eight men in 380 innings.

Wondrous hurler that he was, he was also a good player at bat. He set a hitting and run-scoring pace for all big-league pitchers by smashing 638 hits and scoring 328 runs.

By the time Cy Young reached the end of his particular glory road, he had become a legend. His 511 victories were split between the 291 won in the National League and the 220 he won in the American. When his career ended, Cy Young was forty-four years old, and it wasn't the rubber arm that failed him. He had grown fat and had a substantial paunch.

On a blistering hot afternoon in the 1911 season, he lost a grueling 1–0 hurling duel to a sensational rookie half his age. Leathery-faced Cy Young sighed deeply and remarked to his manager, who was trying to console him:

"Skip, the boys are taking unfair advantage of the old man. Instead of swinging at my stuff, they are laying the ball down, because they know this big stomach of mine makes it hard for me to field their bunts. It's time for me to quit."

He did. He never again pitched in the majors. He went back to his farm in Ohio, milked cows, fed hogs and chickens and played checkers. He remained a fine figure of a man until 1955, when he died at the age of eighty-eight.

The greatest pitcher that ever lived is certainly not forgotten. He is still setting the pace for all big-league hurlers. Now, at the end of every baseball season, the Cy Young Memorial Award is given to each league's outstanding pitcher. It is, naturally, the highest and most coveted honor a pitcher can win, and it is named after the most winning pitcher of them all.

CHRISTY MATHEWSON

FROM AN IDOL TO AN IDEAL

BORN: Christopher Mathewson
        August 12, 1880, Factoryville, Pennsylvania
DIED: October 7, 1925, Saranac Lake, New York
HEIGHT: 6'1½"   WEIGHT: 195 lbs.
Threw and batted right-handed
Lifetime pitching record (17 years): won 373, lost 188, .665

U ndoubtedly the most gentlemanly ballplayer ever to enter the Hall of Fame was Christopher Mathewson. Matty the Great — in an era of roughneck baseball, peopled mostly by unschooled, foul-mouthed, hard-drinking rowdies — was a paragon of virtue. He neither smoked, drank, swore, nor brawled.

Yet despite this refinement, which could be considered a handicap, Christy Mathewson after seventeen years in the big leagues had compiled an astonishing record of 373 victories, the most ever turned in by a National League pitcher. Almost all major-league managers of his time tabbed him as the "greatest pitcher who ever lived." In addition he became the first professional athlete to be worshipped by all young boys in America. He was the country's first great sports idol, the hero of countless millions.

Matty came by his gentility naturally. He was born in the small Pennsylvania farm town of Factoryville to deeply religious parents. They hoped that he would grow up to become a minister in the service of God. While attending Bucknell University, a handsome, blond, open-faced, broad-shouldered six-footer, he captured everyone's

admiration. He was an honor student, president of his class, a member of literary societies and the glee club. He was also an outstanding college football and basketball player.

He was twenty when in 1900 he became a major-league pitcher for the New York Giants who signed him for only $1,500. From the start he knew greatness, although he was ridiculed a good deal by the rowdies because of his status as major-league baseball's first college graduate. But he was a winner from the beginning, for he had everything — strength (they called him Big Six because of his impressive size), intelligence, grace, courage and a fierce competitive will to win.

Matty won twenty or more games a season thirteen times, twelve of those in succession. Four times he won thirty or more, three in a row, and he set a modern National League record by winning thirty-seven in 1908. This record still stands.

One reason for his success was his uncanny control. One year in 416 innings pitched, he walked only forty-two batters. Another time he pitched 306 innings and gave up only twenty-one walks. In 1913, he went sixty-eight consecutive innings without issuing a base on balls — a record for control pitching that may never be matched.

When Matty joined the Giants, they were a last-place club. He pitched them to five pennants. In 1905, his first World Series, he performed the greatest hurling feat in series history. Within a period of five days, he won three complete games — and each victory was a shutout.

Aided by his fantastic "fadeaway," a pitch likened to today's screwball (it broke in on right-handed batters), Big Six pitched two no-hitters during his glorious career. In hurling 634 games, he struck out 2,505 men and walked only 837 (in 4,781 innings) — a record that still hasn't been equaled.

However, what Christy Mathewson brought to the game was something more than pitching greatness. He set a pattern for the conduct of future ballplayers. He brought a touch of class to early major leagues. By the force of his sterling character he made the rough-and-tumble rowdies of that day lift their sights. He earned their respect by his own scrupulous behavior, both on and off the field. Both his teammates and rival players respected and admired him, even idolized him for his thoughtful acts, his unselfishness, his modesty, his sense of honor. As a man of strong religious beliefs, he never pitched on Sunday, a position which his manager and teammates respected. He was so honest that even umpires often took his word on close or doubtful decisions.

In 1916, he was traded to Cincinnati in order that the Reds could make him manager, a post he held until 1918 when at the age of thirty-eight he answered the call to duty and joined the United States military service. He served his country in the First World War. He returned home with his lungs weakened by poison gas, which made him an easy prey for tuberculosis.

In early October, 1925 — while baseball's biggest show, the World Series, was going on — the incomparable right-hander died, at the early age of 45. A nation mourned for him.

When Christy Mathewson entered the Hall of Fame in 1936, it was no surprise. Everyone knew that his immortality had long been assured. At the foot of the plaque which recounts his amazing career there is one line: MATTY WAS MASTER OF THEM ALL.

That he was, but he was even more. The memory of the first genuine gentleman of the major leagues will never fade away. He left his imprint on the game. He brought to baseball intelligence, refinement, dignity, honor and sportsmanship — qualities that lifted the game to a glory worthy of a national pastime.

WALTER JOHNSON

THE FASTEST BIG TRAIN

BORN: Walter Perry Johnson
November 6, 1887, Humboldt, Kansas
DIED: December 10, 1946, Washington, D.C.
HEIGHT: 6'1"   WEIGHT: 200 lbs.
Threw and batted right-handed
Lifetime pitching average (21 years): won 416, lost 279, .599

Among the countless memorable achievements credited to Walter Johnson in his remarkable twenty-one-year career in the major leagues is the unique fact that only he ever pitched in as many as fourteen Opening Day games, and only he ever won nine of them; only he ever performed in Openers before four different presidents of the United States. The man who was to become the swiftest pitcher baseball ever knew pitched his first Opening Day game, on April 15, 1910, when he was twenty-two years old.

It was a historic day for big-league baseball, for among the spectators in the Washington, D.C., ball park was William Howard Taft, the twenty-seventh president of the United States. It marked the first time that a president had graced a major-league ball park with his presence, and it also inaugurated the American tradition of a president's "throwing out the first ball" in an Opener of a new big-league baseball season. This annual baseball custom has been followed by all presidents to this day.

On that memorable day, young Walter Johnson rose to the occa-

94

sion as he did so often in his career by spinning a magnificent one-hit shutout victory. Subsequently, only Johnson pitched Openers before three other presidents of the United States — Woodrow Wilson, Warren Harding and Calvin Coolidge — and he won at least one Opening Day game for each chief executive. Sixteen years later, on April 13, 1926, when he was thirty-nine, Walter Johnson pitched his final Opening Day game in the majors, again in a "command performance" before a president of the United States, and again he gave a memorable display of his hurling greatness. He went fifteen innings to win an Opener again by a shutout. Between his first and last Opening Day triumphs, only he ever won seven Openers by shut-outs.

Walter Johnson was born on a farm in Humboldt, Kansas, to German-Scottish parents. He grew into a big, rawboned youth of sizable proportions. He was nineteen, pitching for a semipro sandlot baseball team in Weiser, Idaho, when he was discovered by a travel-ing cigar salesman who also happened to be an avid baseball fan. Enthusiastically, the traveling salesman alerted every major-league club with glowing reports of the unknown wonder pitcher he had found who hurled baseballs with a speed attained by no mere mortal.

Only the lowly Washington Senators, a chronic major-league losing team, evinced interest. In 1907, they brought the angular farm boy pitcher to the big leagues for the price of a railroad ticket — nine dollars. Walter Johnson remained to shine as a superstar for the Washington Senators until the end of the 1927 season.

His greatness was apparent from the beginning. Throwing with a pendulum arm that propelled a baseball as if it were coming from a slingshot, rookie Johnson tormented and awed major-league batters with fast balls, difficult to see and almost impossible to hit. They said he had only two pitches — fast and faster.

While still a rookie, Johnson performed an incredible feat that was to set the pattern for the greatness that was to be his. Within the time of only four days, he pitched an entire three-game series for his team, winning all three by shutouts. Because he delivered a baseball from the mound to home plate faster than any other pitcher in history, he was nicknamed the Big Train and how that big train roared on the glory road, down through the baseball years.

Though for most of his major-league time, Walter Johnson pitched for a Washington club of inept and mediocre players, he accom-plished a host of heroic feats that set him apart from all other pitching wonders in baseball history. He won 20 or more games a season no less than twelve times, ten in a row. Twice he won 30 or more games a season, back-to-back. Over that two-year period, he won 68 games for his lowly team. One season he won 16 games in a row. And once, he hurled fifty-six consecutive scoreless innings for an American League record that still stands. His pitching was of such astonishing pinpoint quality that in his 802 major-league games, he averaged less than two walks a game.

He became the only pitcher of the twentieth century to hurl 531 complete major-league games. Only he ever hurled as many as 113 shutouts, and only he ever accomplished the incredible feat of striking out as many as 3,508 major-league batters. He did it in 5,924 innings. In all, he won 416 games. Moreover, he accepted the most fielding chances and posted the best fielding average of any hurler in big-league history.

He was the all-American sports hero in every sense, and it was no wonder that he was the favorite baseball player of United States presidents who placed him on a pedestal. In addition to this stupendous and awesome talent, Walter Johnson lived a life of purity that was an example for every boy in America. His nobility, modesty, and decency shone through everything he did. He was the perfect sportsman who took his triumphs with supreme grace. He never smoked, drank or swore. Even under extreme pressure, his wildest profane utterance was: "Goodness gracious sakes alive."

Incomparable pitcher though Walter Johnson was, he waited eighteen years before he finally saw action in a World Series. He was thirty-seven years old when the Washington Senators finally won their first American League pennant. That seesaw 1924 World Series dragged out to seven games, and the final contest ended in the twelfth inning, with the famed Big Train on the mound — the winner. Walter Johnson's first World Series pitching victory created such a wave of sentiment throughout the nation that grown men actually cried with tears of joy, and there was dancing in the streets by his many happy admirers.

Walter Johnson was enshrined in the Hall of Fame in 1936. When he died, ten years later, the entire nation mourned for him. His memory has been kept alive in many unique and noble ways. Annually, in Washington, D.C., a special ceremony is held before Walter Johnson's monument. Streets have been named in his honor. There is a Walter Johnson baseball league in which thousands of youngsters participate. In Bethesda, Maryland, there is a Walter Johnson High School. It is the only educational institution in the world named in honor of a big-league baseball player.

His bronze plaque in baseball's Hall of Fame now has a simple inscription to identify him: "Walter Perry Johnson. . . . Conceded to be Fastest Ball Pitcher In History Of The Game."

He was that — and a lot more.

PETE ALEXANDER

ALEX THE GREAT

BORN: Grover Cleveland Alexander
    February 26, 1887, Elba, Nebraska
DIED: November 4, 1950, St. Paul, Nebraska
HEIGHT: 6'   WEIGHT: 185 lbs.
Threw and batted right-handed
Lifetime record (20 years): won 373, lost 208, .642

Grover Cleveland Alexander was everything a great pitcher could possibly be, and yet he was also everything a big-league pitcher shouldn't be. He was undisciplined, irresponsible, alcoholic, epileptic, and his own worst enemy. But above all, he was incredible, one of the greatest major-league pitchers ever.

Incredible Alex started life on a shabby Nebraska farm, in a family of thirteen children, twelve of them boys. A gangling freckle-faced, sandy-haired farm boy, he was twenty-four when he finally came to the big leagues to pitch. In 1911, the Philadelphia Phillies, desperately in need of an extra hurler, had purchased him from a minor-league club, for a paltry $750. He proved an immediate sensation, for as a rookie pitcher he won twenty-eight games. No hurler in history has ever matched Alexander's record of victories in his first major-league season.

Pitching with effortless grace, uncanny control, and deadly efficiency, he soon earned the sobriquet of Alexander the Great.

To enrich his ever-growing fame as one of the most incredible pitchers ever, he created awesome mound masterpieces. In 1915, his thirty-one victories sparked the Philadelphia Phillies to their first National League pennant. For three consecutive seasons, Alex won more than thirty games a year.

As the baseball seasons passed, Alexander the Great pitched in more major-league games than any other hurler in the history of the National League — 696. No pitcher in history ever exceeded his record of sixteen shutouts in a season, nor has any pitcher in National League history ever matched his lifetime total of ninety shutouts. So magnificent and durable a mound artist was Alexander that at times he pitched both ends of doubleheaders. Twice he won both ends of doubleheaders.

In 1918, when Alexander the Great was at the height of his fame as a pitching marvel, he left the majors to shoulder a rifle for the United States Army. But when he returned to the major leagues to pitch again, he was sick due to exposure to poison gas. He became a ballplayer vulnerable to sudden epileptic seizures.

But he was still Alexander the Great, for after the Philadelphia club traded him to the Chicago Cubs, in the nine years he pitched for Chicago, he never had a losing season.

Because of his inclination to break training, his indifference to his fame, and his undisciplined behavior, Alexander found it difficult to remain with any team for too long a time. In 1926, he was traded to the St. Louis Cardinals, and though he was then thirty-nine, his efficient hurling promptly helped them win the National League pennant.

However, in that memorable World Series against the once mighty New York Yankees, Old Pete, as he was then called, proved why he was Alexander the Great. For in that classic, he produced his finest hour as one of the best pitchers ever.

At age 39, Alexander had pitched and won two games in the 1926 World Series. He seemed to have completed his hurling chores for the classic. But in the seventh inning of the seventh and final game, with the bases full and the dangerous Yankee slugger Tony Lazzeri at bat, the Cardinals' manager called Old Pete in to relieve the faltering St. Louis pitcher and protect a slim one-run lead.

In trudged weary old Alexander from the bullpen. He took a few warmup pitches to crank up his aged right arm, then fanned Tony Lazzeri, and went on to save the game and the World Series championship for the St. Louis Cardinals. In his fantastic twenty-year career in the majors, Alexander the Great struck out 2,199 men. Yet ironically this is the one strikeout that will never be forgotten.

When incredible Alex turned forty, he was still a great enough mound master to post twenty-one victories for a season. No other pitcher in National League history ever won more games than Alexander the Great. He won 373!

He was past forty-three when he finally departed from the majors and his life was all downhill from there on. The man who was once named for a president of the United States came to a pathetic finish as a baseball hero. For a while, to survive, Grover Cleveland Alexander became a freak attraction in a flea circus where he reminisced of his great pitching days. Finally, he drifted home where he died in a shabby rented room in a small Nebraska town. He passed from the world alone and friendless, far from the roaring crowd that once hailed him as Alexander the Great.

But he departed with the knowledge that his greatness as a pitcher would always be remembered. For he entered baseball's Hall of Fame and joined the other honored immortals of the national pastime.

SANDY KOUFAX

MIRACLE HURLER

BORN: Sanford Braun
      December 30, 1935, Brooklyn, New York
HEIGHT: 6'2"   WEIGHT: 198 lbs.
Threw left-handed and batted right-handed
Lifetime pitching record (12 years): won 165, lost 87, .655

In 1972, when Sandy Koufax entered the Hall of Fame as one of the most dazzling pitchers of all time, he was only thirty-six years old — the youngest player ever enshrined at Cooperstown. It was most incredible that he ever reached there at all, for when he broke into the major leagues in 1955, amused skeptics had said, "Why, he throws just like a girl."

And for the first six years of his big-league career, it appeared that the skeptics were right. He lost more games (forty) than he won (thirty-six) and his earned-run average soared over four runs a game. He could have been described as a major-league flop.

But then at age twenty-five, Sandy Koufax began performing such incredible winning feats that baseball historians acclaimed him the equal of any pitching great that ever lived. In the following six years, he won 129 games and lost only 47, led the league in strikeouts four times, set an all-time strikeout record of 382 for one season, and was named Most Valuable Player, Major League Player of the Year and (four times) National League Pitcher of the Year. He won the Cy Young Award, emblematic of the league's best pitcher, three times — the only hurler ever so honored.

Then, though only thirty-one years old, Koufax quit the game and thus ended the legend of the paradoxical baseball hero who never wanted to be what he had become.

He was born Sanford Braun in a middle-class area of Brooklyn. His parents were divorced when he was a child. As Sandy grew older, he came to be known by the name of his stepfather — Koufax. A serious, shy and well-mannered boy, Sandy never expected nor wanted to be a baseball player. He had no enthusiasm for the game. His greatest joy as an athlete was playing basketball. A star for his high school team, he was so good at that game that he was given a basketball scholarship to the University of Cincinnati.

He went out for baseball in college only because his basketball coach also coached baseball. Back at home in Brooklyn, Sandy had played sandlot baseball just to be with his friends. Because he was a poor fielder and a weak hitter as a first baseman, he made the team as pitcher. He could throw fast and hard, although most of the time he didn't know where the pitches were going.

It came as a surprise to Sandy that his pitching in college drew the attention of a big-league scout. The Brooklyn Dodgers lured him off the campus with a $14,000 bonus and a promise of a $6,000 annual salary. He was nineteen when, in 1955, he came to the majors to pitch.

At first he was scared, uncomfortable and embarrassed because he didn't even know how to stand on the mound, or how signs were given in the big leagues. He was so nervous and tense that a kindly Dodger coach advised him to practice his pitching in private.

He made his first start in the majors on July 6, 1955. In four innings he walked eight batters, and for the whole season barely managed to win two games. The following season he was no better, again winning only two of his outings. Sandy wanted to quit the game and go back to college. "I don't enjoy making a fool of myself. I really don't belong in the majors," he told his manager. But the Dodgers had faith in him and they raised his salary to $7,000 a year — and he stayed on.

When the club left Brooklyn to settle in Los Angeles, Koufax was still a flop on the mound. His speed was still devastating, as demonstrated by his mounting strikeout total, but he was still a loser. However, one August night in 1959 he gave a glimpse of things to come when he amazed a record crowd of 82,794 by striking out eighteen batters in a nine-inning game — then a modern-day mark.

Two years later, Sandy stopped trying to throw the ball past hitters. He harnessed his blazing fast ball and worked on control, curves and change-ups. He won eighteen games in 1961 and was on his way to glory as a superstar.

The following year, he again struck out eighteen batters in a game (the only pitcher in history to do it twice) and he registered his first no-hit, no-run game. In midseason, after he had won fourteen games, he ran into misfortune due to an injury that nearly ended his career. A bruise on his left hand turned some of his fingers numb and they lost their sense of touch. Doctors diagnosed his condition as Reynaud's phenomenon, a circulatory ailment resulting from a blood clot in his palm. He won no more games that season, but medication and rest cured the ailment which, Sandy later learned, could have caused loss of a finger on his pitching hand.

In 1963, when baseball people were wondering what lay in store for Koufax, he staged the most unbelievable comeback ever achieved by a major-league pitcher. He was as overpowering as any pitcher ever. He led the league in strikeouts (306), a new league record. He led both leagues in shutouts (11). He led the majors in earned-run average with 1.88, and he also pitched the second no-hitter of his career. His twenty-five victories led the Los Angeles Dodgers to a pennant.

Incredible as Sandy was during that season, he attained new heights in the World Series. In winning the first game, he set a new all-time record by striking out fifteen New York Yankee hitters. He added eight more strikeouts while winning the fourth game — completing a four-game sweep of the then mighty Bronx Bombers, for the world championship.

Early in 1964, Sandy pitched his third no-hit, no-run game. After winning nineteen games that season, he was again ambushed by hard luck. While sliding into a base, he injured his left elbow and was sidelined for the year, a damaging blow to the Dodgers' hopes for another pennant. And the worst was yet to come. Sandy discovered to his horror that he had developed traumatic arthritis in his left elbow.

When the 1965 season started, Sandy was resigned to living with his handicapped elbow. The Dodgers expected to use him as, possibly, a once-a-week starter. But, despite the pain involved, Sandy again astonished the baseball world with another unbelievable comeback.

Though hurling with an uncertain arm, both a physical and a

mental strain for Sandy that year since he knew that his arthritic elbow could flare up and end his career at any time, he still recorded the most remarkable season of glory that ever blessed a major-league pitching great.

He did not miss a pitching start all year. He hurled more innings than any other pitcher in the majors (336) and he completed more games than anyone else (twenty-seven). His twenty-six victories paced all pitchers in both major leagues. He set a new all-time record for strikeouts in a season by fanning 382 batters, an astonishing mark inasmuch as the previous big-league record was 343 for a left-hander (set in 1904) and 348 for a right-hander (set in 1946).

And, in addition, he reached a pitching pinnacle achieved by only five others in the twentieth century: He pitched a perfect no-hit, no-run game, which represented his fourth career no-hitter, to become the first and only hurler in history ever to achieve that magical feat.

His unmatched pitching led the Dodgers to another pennant. He climaxed that superb season with two decisive shutout victories in the World Series to lead his team again to the world championship. Again he won the Cy Young Award for being the greatest mounds-man in the majors.

That superlative year won him a place in sports history, for he became the highest-paid ballplayer of all time. He was signed to a salary of $135,000 for the 1966 season — and at the end of the year nobody could say that he wasn't worth every penny.

Even with the crooked arthritic left elbow causing him extreme discomfort (he had to pack it in ice to relieve the pain after every game), Koufax pitched through that entire 1966 season as no left-hander in the history of baseball ever had done before.

He won 27 games, an all-time season's record for a southpaw pitcher in the National League. He pitched the most innings (323), completed the most games (27) and made the most starts (41). He led the league in earned-run average with 1.73 — the fifth consecutive year he had captured that honor. It was a new all-time major league record.

Also, he led the league in strikeouts with 317, the third season in succession that he had struck out 300 or more men — a feat achieved by no other big-leaguer in the twentieth century. Again he led the Dodgers to a pennant, and again he won the coveted Cy Young Award as the majors' greatest pitcher — for an unprecedented third time. By the end of the 1966 season, Sandy Koufax had overwhelming credentials to verify his fame as a pitching immortal. He had struck out ten or more batters in a major-league game for an all-time record of 97 times. He had recorded at least one strikeout for every inning he had pitched in the major leagues — for a career total of 2,396 plus 61 more strikeouts in World Series competition.

But as the awards and records piled up, Sandy, incredibly, turned his back on the game before the 1967 baseball season began. Sadly, but without regret, he told a stunned baseball world:

"I've decided to retire because I don't want to go on when I can't any more. I don't want to maim myself pitching with my arthritic elbow, and perhaps wind up with an arm I won't be able to use for the rest of my life."

So he quit the major leagues as a pitcher, at age thirty-one.

But he left the game as a legend in his own lifetime. Even though he won only 165 games in his injury-shortened, late-started major-league career (129 of them won in his last six years), there was never a doubt that he would reach the Hall of Fame. For wherever baseball is played and revered, that once magnificent slim left-hander known as Sandy Koufax will always be remembered for his courage, ideals, sportsmanship, and fantastic pitching feats. The boy who had never wanted to play baseball, and who in the beginning of his big-league career was ridiculed for "throwing a ball like a girl" left the game as a Hall of Fame superman of the mound.

RUBE WADDELL

GLORIOUS SCREWBALL

BORN: George Edward Waddell
      October 13, 1876, Bradford, Pennsylvania
DIED: April 1, 1914, San Antonio, Texas
HEIGHT: 6'1"   WEIGHT: 196 lbs.
Threw and batted left-handed.
Lifetime pitching record (14 years): won 191, lost 142, .574

No sport has boasted as many eccentrics, screwballs, zanies, oddballs, loons, and clowns, intentionally or otherwise, as big-league baseball. The legendary Rube Waddell set the pace for them all. Because of him the belief was born that all baseball left-handers are a breed apart.

In 1897, George Edward (Rube) Waddell came to the big leagues from Bradford, Pennsylvania, a tall, powerful, deep-chested, long-armed, twenty-one-year-old country boy. In the thirteen years he remained in the majors, he pitched for five different clubs: Louisville, Pittsburgh, Chicago, Philadelphia, and St. Louis; managers wearied of his eccentricities and let him drift away for their own peace of mind. Only the wise and patient Connie Mack could handle him with any degree of success. In the five and a half seasons that the erratic left-hander pitched for the immortal Connie Mack and his Philadelphia Athletics, despite all his clowning and weird capers, he averaged twenty-two victories a season and never had fewer than 200 strikeouts in any of those seasons. He won 131 games.

When screwball Waddell was in shape, and could be made to attend strictly to the serious business of pitching, he was a matchless performer. He was the equal of any pitcher who ever lived. For he had an incomparable combination of awesome speed and bewildering curves. He was virtually unhittable.

But pitching always came last with baseball's greatest clown, who had the brains and charm of a little boy. No pitching assignment was important enough ever to prevent him from fishing, chasing fire engines, marching in parades, tending bar, drinking, and participating in the looniest capers.

He would often turn cartwheels when going from the pitcher's mound to the bench. During games, he would vanish from the ball park in pursuit of clanging fire engines on the way to a fire. Sometimes he would sneak out between innings for a quick visit to a neighboring tavern to trade an autographed baseball for a drink. He never missed marching in a parade if there was one going on in town. Often on the way to the ball park he would stop to play marbles with children or become involved in a sandlot baseball game with happy youngsters.

Once his distraught manager found him in a department store window posing as a clothing dummy to attract and amuse pedestrians passing by. Another time, his horrified manager discovered that he had hired himself out as a performer in a side show, wrestling live alligators for a dollar a performance.

Once, to win a small wager, Rube Waddell leaped out of a two-story window. Another time on a dare, he jumped from a ferry boat into icy water to swim miles back to shore. Once, when his team was involved in a torrid pennant race, southpaw Waddell disappeared for ten days and hid out in an obscure little fishing town where he fished to his heart's content.

Training rules and curfew hours had no meaning for Rube Waddell. He gave the baseball world a million laughs. He was an enormous drawing card, for he was a colorful and overpowering pitcher with a fantastic rubber left arm that mowed down batters as fast as they came to the plate. He became something of a folk hero.

Once he pitched every game of a six-game series against the Detroit Tigers, and he won five of them. In the 407 major-league games he appeared in, the southpaw Rube struck out 10 or more men in a game sixty times. In 1908, he struck out 16 men in a nine-inning game, and it stood as a record for years. In 1904, he whiffed 343 batters; forty-three years were to pass before that strikeout record was topped. His control was the finest ever known in a southpaw. Erratic as he was, he could think quickly and clearly in a baseball uniform. In his short but hilarious stay in the big leagues, baseball's greatest clown still managed to win 191 games and strike out 2,375 batters.

Early in 1912, the irresponsible left-hander was on a visit to Hickman, Kentucky, when the Mississippi River rose and threatened the panic-stricken town with inundation. The levee had broken.

Without hesitation, famous Rube Waddell joined the army of volunteer workers building safeguards. For hours he stood in icy water up to his armpits, piling sacks of sand in place. He paid a costly price for his heroic contribution. He was left with a severe cold and a racking cough. He later developed tuberculosis.

He was never the same powerful pitcher again, although he clowned all the way. Hurling became too much of a physical strain for him, and eventually he wound up in a sanitarium fighting for his life. The two-hundred-pound Rube shrank to a hundred pounds. He was only thirty-seven when he died. Ironically, it came on April 1, 1914, the traditional April Fool's Day. Perhaps it was an appropriate time for baseball's greatest clown to depart from this world.

A six-foot shaft of granite, topped with a baseball, was placed as a monument over his grave in San Antonio, Texas. But the most eccentric, most incorrigible, and greatest screwball of America's national pastime had an even more glowing and lasting memorial to his fame as a big-league pitching wonder. Thirty-two years later, Rube Waddell had the last laugh; he became the first genuine diamond clown in major-league history to be elected to the Hall of Fame.

MORDECAI BROWN

THREE FINGERS TO FAME

BORN: Mordecai Peter Brown
October 19, 1876, Nyesville, Indiana
DIED: February 14, 1948, Terre Haute, Indiana
HEIGHT: 5'10"   WEIGHT: 175 lbs.
Threw right-handed and batted both ways
Lifetime pitching average (14 years): won 239, lost 130, .631

Because he was born in 1876, just one hundred years after the Declaration of Independence established the free and equal United States of America, and because his parents were deeply religious and fervently patriotic, he was christened Mordecai Peter Centennial Brown. But throughout his entire baseball career, he was simply called Three-Fingered Brown. That name became a legend. He was the only big-league ballplayer in history who used a crippled and deformed hand to gain entrance to baseball's Hall of Fame.

When Brown was only a five-year-old, chubby-faced, jovial boy, misfortune fell. While visiting a farm one day, his childish curiosity prompted him to poke his right hand into a threshing machine. In that accident, he lost half of his index finger. The stump healed leaving a large knot on the end of it.

A year later, young Mordecai again was the victim of an accident. While chasing an animal in a stubby field, running as fast as his little legs could carry him, he stumbled, fell, and broke two fingers of his

113

right hand. The country doctor didn't do a very good job on Brown's injured hand, for when his two broken fingers healed, they remained stiff and twisted. He grew up with three deformed fingers and for the rest of his life he had to live with a crippled and gnarled right hand.

As he grew older, young Brown tried to play baseball even though his deformed fingers made it difficult for him to grip a ball with his right hand. However, he developed a great love for the game and he had only one ambition. He wanted to be a baseball player.

At the age of fifteen because of family needs, he went underground to toil in the mines. He hated that work and dreamed only of playing baseball in the sunshine. A bit of luck came his way to brighten his dreary young life.

A timekeeper at the mine called Legs O'Connell, a onetime professional baseball player, took a liking to the youngster with the deformed right hand and undertook the job of tutoring him in baseball play. Each day after work he would have Brown practice throwing the ball, and he taught him how to grip it to make the best use of his four-and-a-half fingers. He was a hard teacher, but he taught Brown how to overcome the handicap of his crippled fingers and put them to great advantage. However, when Brown threw a ball, it would often jump in unpredictable ways.

"Don't let that bother you," instructor Legs O'Connell would tell Brown. "That stump of a finger on your right hand may be worth a fortune to you some day."

Finally, there came a day when Legs O'Connell convinced the manager of a small-town professional team to give Brown a chance on the mound to pitch. He was twenty-two then and he was paid a salary of two dollars a day when his team played. Brown did so well that all the puzzled batters who faced his unusual pitches wondered what in the world "the freak with the deformed hand" was throwing at them. Soon, he came to be known in bush-league baseball as Three-Fingered Brown.

However, it wasn't until he was twenty-six that he finally came to the big leagues as a pitcher. He broke in with the St. Louis Cardinals in 1903, and as a rookie with a last-place team, he won nine games while losing thirteen. But after only one season with that mediocre team, he was traded to the Chicago Cubs, then in their glory as an outstanding major-league team, for they featured the legendary Tinker-to-Evers-to-Chance infield. Three-Fingered Brown quickly reached his peak as an outstanding major-league pitcher. Whenever he pitched for the Cubs, opposing batters continually hit his baffling deliveries into the ground for baseball's greatest infield to scoop up for easy outs. With his deformed right hand and masterful down-curve, Three-Fingered Brown revolutionized the art of baffling pitching.

In his glory years with the Chicago Cubs, he not only outpitched the greatest pitchers of his time, but he became one of the greatest winning hurlers in major-league history. Season after season he won more than twenty games, and he was a "workhorse-hurler" for the Cubs who always drew the toughest pitching assignments. Within a period of only five seasons (1906–1910) Three-Fingered Brown pitched the Cubs to four National League pennants and two world championships. He won five World Series games, three of them by shutouts. But there never was a day that Brown didn't have pain in his pitching hand while toiling on the mound.

That amazing hurler, with the deformed pitching hand which threw the weirdest curves that ever hoodwinked big-league batsmen, starred in the major leagues for fourteen years. The record book shows that he pitched fifty-two shutouts, and won 239 games against only 130 losses.

The three gnarled fingers of his right hand were sufficient to make Mordecai Brown one of the pitching wonders of major-league history, and earn for him an honored place in the Hall of Fame. They also enriched baseball history with an inspiring story of unbelievable courage.

WARREN SPAHN

SOUTHPAW MAGICIAN

BORN: Warren Edward Spahn,
       April 23, 1921, Buffalo, New York
HEIGHT: 6′   WEIGHT: 183 lbs.
Threw and batted left-handed
Lifetime record (20 years): won 363, lost 245, .597

I n 1973, the magnificent bronze doors of the Baseball Hall of Fame swung wide open to admit the 135th member of the Cooperstown shrine, as great a baseball hero as had ever played the game. Warren Spahn warranted his glory for he was a genuine phenomenon — the winningest and greatest left-handed pitcher of all time.

The son of a humble wallpaper salesman who once had been an obscure semipro baseball player, Warren began throwing and catching a baseball, under his father's tutorship, before he even had learned the alphabet. By the age of nine, he was the star first baseman for a midget baseball team, and by thirteen, he was starring at first base for the Lake City Athletic Club in Buffalo, a baseball team of grown men. His father played third base for that team. The Spahn father-and-son infield combination was the sensation of the Buffalo sandlots.

At South Park High, Spahn switched to left-handed pitching. He became so outstanding as a schoolboy hurler that a baseball scout offered him a contract from a big league team. Overjoyed, young Warren was willing to become an instant school dropout to play pro

117

baseball. But to his surprise, his father insisted that he complete his high school education.

"More than anything else in the world I want to see you become a big league ballplayer," said his father, "but this is not the time for you to start. Finish school then whatever you want to do, I won't object. I have confidence in you that you will make it in the big leagues."

Warren Spahn listened to his father's advice, and remained in high school. But as soon as he had graduated, he signed with the Boston Braves to pitch for their Bradford farm club at $250 a month.

From the start of his pro baseball career, he was plagued by misfortune. He tore tendons in his left shoulder and was sidelined, and when he resumed pitching, a painful arm ailment forced him to quit again. After a long rest, when he returned to pitching, again he was a victim of misfortune. For a thrown baseball broke his nose, and disfigured him for life.

Warren was twenty-one years old when he finally came to the big leagues to pitch for the Boston Braves. But before he could win even one game in the major leagues, he vanished from the big-time baseball scene, for almost four years. In all the time he was away from the majors, he was an American soldier fighting for his country in the European battle zones of World War II. He was wounded in the historic bloody Battle of the Bulge.

But he survived, and returned to the Boston Braves in 1946, decorated with a Bronze Star, a Purple Heart and a Presidential Citation, plus jittery nerves. It wasn't until he was twenty-five that he finally won his first game as a major-league pitcher. That season, Warren Spahn barely managed to win eight games.

However, the following season that slender, sleek and stylish left-hander blossomed out as a hurling artist of amazing control, guile, and workhorse durability. He achieved his first season as a twenty-game winner, and was so remarkable that he continued to win twenty or more games a season, thirteen times in all. It was a feat achieved by no other southpaw pitcher in major league history.

As the seasons passed, when it came to pitching, nothing was too farfetched for "Spahnie" to achieve. Eight times, he led the National League in victories, and nine times in pitching the most complete games — a major-league record. For seventeen consecutive seasons, he struck out more than 100 batters, for another major-league record. In all, he registered the most strikeouts ever achieved by a left-handed pitcher, 2,583. He also pitched the most innings ever hurled by a major-league southpaw — 5,246 with 63 shutouts.

Three times his extraordinary pitching won a pennant for his team, and four times he registered victories in the World Series. He was the only pitcher in National League history to hit as many as 35 home runs for his fame. And only he ever started as many as 665 major-league games.

In 1960, when Warren Spahn was crowding forty, he pitched his first no-hit, no-run game of his fabulous major-league career.

"It's ridiculous for a man of my age to pitch a no-hitter," said a jubilant Warren Spahn, still taken aback by the incongruity of that feat. So, one season later, he pitched his second no-hitter. He was so remarkable that he was a twenty-three-game winner when he was forty-two years old.

Once, John F. Kennedy, then the president of the United States, paid Warren Spahn an unusual honor in tribute to his fame as the greatest left-handed pitcher in baseball history, when he said:

"You have been one of the few men in the history of baseball who established new records of achievement and new historic landmarks whenever you played. Your unbroken years of success have been a testimony of your strength of character, competitive zeal, and physical stamina. Few athletes in our time have won the national admiration which you have."

When Warren Spahn was nearing his forty-fifth birthday, he finally reached the end of his long journey on the glory road, as a major-league pitcher. By that time, he had firmly established himself as the winningest and greatest left-handed pitcher of all time. For he left the big leagues with 363 victories.

But he never stopped wanting to win. In 1973, the balding, hawk-nosed left-handed pitching wonder achieved his greatest victory on the glory mound when the magnificent bronze doors of the Baseball Hall of Fame swung wide open to welcome him for enshrinement as a genuine baseball immortal. For as long as baseball lives, so long will live the name of pitcher Warren Spahn.

WHITEY FORD

FAIR-HAIRED BIG CITY BOY

BORN: Edward Charles Ford
        October 21, 1928, New York, New York
HEIGHT: 5' 10"   WEIGHT: 181 lbs.
Threw and batted left-handed
Lifetime record (16 years): won 236, lost 106, .690

In 1974, when southpaw Whitey Ford had his last "hurrah" as a pitching great in his enshrinement in the Hall of Fame, he entered the pantheon of baseball gods with a number of accomplishments unknown to any other pitching immortal. He possessed for his glory the best and highest won-lost lifetime pitching percentage in all major league history — .690. Also, he was the winningest pitcher in World Series history. His achievements as a World Series hurling hero may never be equaled.

Whitey Ford's glorious journey to Hall of Fame immortality began on the sidewalks of New York. Born in a shabby tenement district of the world's largest city, Whitey gained his first pitching skills on the paved streets of Manhattan and the sandlots within reach of his midtown home. As he grew older, he became a star pitcher for his high school team. A cocky, wisecracking and confident big-city youngster, Whitey had no doubts that his destiny was to become a famous big-league pitcher.

As soon as he graduated from high school, he appeared for a tryout with the fabulous New York Yankees. He was one of forty other ambitious boys from all over the country who had come for that Yankees' tryout session. But Whitey Ford attracted little attention and interest as a pitching prospect for the big leagues. He went home disappointed but still confident and resumed his hurling on the sandlots.

Eventually, three big-league scouts spotted him, and they became so impressed with his southpaw hurling that they began bidding for his services. But two of them quickly bowed out of the picture, whereupon the remaining scout signed Whitey to a New York Yankees' contract, for a $7,000 bonus. He was then nineteen years old.

Whitey was shipped off to a Yankees' farm club for seasoning. He spent 3½ years hurling in the obscurity of the minors, until he took matters into his own hands to gain entrance to the big leagues. In 1950, when the New York Yankees were in a tight pennant race for the American League flag, the Yankees' manager, venerable Casey Stengel, received an unusual telegram. It read: "If you want to win the pennant this season, you had better bring up pitcher Whitey Ford from the minors without delay. He will help win the pennant." It was signed Whitey Ford.

Manager Casey Stengel, who was famed for his unusual big-league doings, was so amused by Whitey Ford's brashness and cocky confidence that he ordered him to report promptly to the parent club. So the twenty-two-year-old Ford finally came to the big leagues to pitch. His major-league debut as a hurler for the Yankees was a flop. In his first appearance on the mound in a major-league game, he was pummeled for five runs in five innings and he walked six rival batters before he was removed from the hill. But he shrugged off that inauspicious beginning as a big-league pitcher with a wisecrack.

"I won't lose again," said cocky Whitey Ford. And he didn't. He reeled off nine victories in a row, for an American League record for most consecutive games won by a rookie pitcher. He also tied a major-league record by hurling two consecutive one-hit games. True to his boast, pitcher Ford helped the Yankees win the 1950 pennant. When he appeared in his first World Series game, he won it, and helped the New York team win the baseball championship of the world in a four-game sweep.

However, the following season the sensational rookie left-hander was no longer in the big leagues. He had entered the United States Army for military service in the Korean War. Whitey was away from the majors for two years, and once he had a close brush with death. But when he returned to the New York Yankees, he promptly resumed his winning ways. For the next thirteen years, he never had a losing season, and he won fame as one of the greatest major-league pitchers of his time. He was a left-handed wizard with a magic arm, a courageous heart and a smart head. On the mound, he was a rugged, cocksure competitor always arrogantly challenging the greatest batters who faced him.

During his sixteen-year tenure as the Yankees' greatest pitcher, Whitey Ford, who became known as the "Chairman of the Board," won 236 games while losing only 106 and compiled the highest winning percentage of all major-league pitchers in history, past and present, with over 100 victories. His lifetime won-lost percentage was an incredible .690! Moreover, his lifetime earned-run average as a major-league pitcher was an unbelievable 2.74 — the best among all the pitching elite of big-league history.

Whitey Ford's hurling magic sparked the New York Yankees to eleven pennants and seven World Series championships. And in World Series combat, the cocky little southpaw established himself as the greatest World Series pitching hero of all time.

Only he in baseball history ever pitched in twenty-two World Series games. Only he ever hurled as many as 146 innings in classic combat, and only he ever struck out ninety-four batters in World Series play. His fantastic feat of hurling 33 World Series shutout innings in a row is an all-time record that may never be equaled. And only Whitey Ford in all baseball history ever won ten World Series games for his glory.

The brilliant big-league saga of southpaw pitcher Whitey Ford came to a sudden and dramatic end when he was crowding age thirty-nine. After he had undergone an operation for circulatory blockage in his left shoulder, he started the 1967 major-league season with doubts about the efficiency of his famed pitching arm. He struggled on the mound until Memorial Day of that season, winning only two games out of seven he had pitched. Then one day during a losing game, courageous Whitey suddenly decided to stop struggling with pain and mediocrity. He walked off the mound and went to the clubhouse. When his teammates returned to the locker room after that game, they discovered that Whitey Ford was gone, as were his clothes and all his locker belongings. He had packed up and gone home — never to return to pitch in the major leagues again.

But the greatest of all baseball triumphs still awaited Whitey Ford. It came in 1974 when he was fifty-four years old. He was enshrined in the Hall of Fame as one of the immortals of the game.

And great, indeed, was his final glory as a pitching wizard for the ages. For as a unique winning hurler and World Series hero, little Whitey Ford towered above all the other pitching immortals in the Hall of Fame.

SATCHEL PAIGE

ROCK OF AGES

BORN: Leroy Robert Paige.
   Believed to have been born July 7, 1906, Mobile, Alabama
HEIGHT: 6'4"   WEIGHT: 190 lbs.
Threw and batted right-handed
Big-league average (6 years): won 28, lost 31

I n the summer of 1948, sports headlines informed a startled baseball world that the Cleveland Indians had hired Leroy (Satchel) Paige to pitch in the major leagues. His arrival on the big-league scene caused strange reactions. Many of baseball's fans vehemently criticized his coming to the majors as a grotesque comedy that demeaned the dignity of the national pastime. Others believed that a rookie pitcher like Paige cast a reflection on the entire scheme of operation in the major leagues. Cynics accused Bill Veeck, then the boss of the Cleveland Indians, of being an incorrigible showman who was exploiting the race issue in baseball purely for profit. For never before had a black man pitched in the major leagues.

However, Paige was not only the first black pitcher in major-league history but also the strangest freshman ever seen in the big leagues. Standing 6 ft., 4 in. tall and weighing barely 175 lbs., he looked like an ancient gnome on stilts and walked like an amiable camel. When he joined the Cleveland Indians on July 17, 1948, he claimed to be thirty-nine years old. But a board of health birth record in Mobile, Alabama, where he was born, revealed that he was

forty-two. His mother was certain that he was forty-four. Friends and neighbors who had known him since boyhood in the South claimed that he was close to fifty.

The question of Satchel Paige's accurate age became baseball's hottest topic of discussion. No one ever found out how old he really was. Nevertheless, he was the oldest rookie in baseball history, and everyone knew that he would become a legend even before he entered the major leagues.

That venerable black hurler when still a mere boy was pitching professionally against baseball teams of grown men. For more than a quarter of a century he had stalked the United States, Canada, and South America, looking for a ball park to pitch in. A self-taught hurler, he had become the most incredible baseball thrower ever known. He performed in all climates and under a wide variety of conditions, mowing down all batters who faced him with monotonous regularity. He pitched more than 100 games each year for more than two decades, and as the years went by, he became the most wondrous barnstorming pitcher of all time. The foremost showman in the game, his earnings as a pitcher amounted to more than $50,000 a year. His travels averaged 30,000 miles a year.

However, although he was rated as one of the wonders of the age, for decades he had been an outcast from the big leagues because of the unwritten rule against blacks in organized baseball. When Satchel Paige's big-league chance finally came and he joined the Cleveland Indians in 1948 as a rookie, he wasn't half the pitcher he had been in his youth and prime. Already, he had pitched about 3,000 pro games, and he had won more than 2,500 of them — 45 no-hit games and 250 shutouts.

Old Satch pitched his very first game in the majors on July 9. It was a two-inning relief job. Six days later, he won his first major-league game, hurling 3⅓ scoreless innings in relief. On August 13, rookie Paige got his first starting assignment. Old as he was, the first black hurler in major-league history pitched a masterpiece — a five-hit shutout against the Chicago White Sox. More than 50,000 fans turned out to see what that ancient right-hander could do as a regular big-league pitcher.

For his second regular pitching start, rookie Paige drew a record crowd of 78,382 spectators. He pitched his greatest game in a big-league uniform. He hurled a three-hit shutout. As worn out as his wondrous pitching arm was, nevertheless he proved a tremendous attraction at the gate. In his first three major-league starts in which he was the advertised pitcher, 201,829 spectators crowded their way into the ball park to watch rookie Paige perform his hurling magic and victimize all the big-league batters who faced him. He proved a golden investment for the Cleveland Indians. For he not only won six crucial games as a starting pitcher, but he saved a score of others in relief, helping his team win the pennant.

With his bewildering pitches, unusual hurling tricks, amazing control, and cleverness, old Satch lasted five seasons in the majors, appeared in 178 games, and struck out close to 300 batters. Officially, he won only twenty-five big-league games, but he saved more than fifty as a relief pitcher.

His brief tenure in the major leagues was a lark for Paige. A nonconformist with many eccentricities, he proved a constant trial to his manager. Pitching in the big time was no serious task for him. He clowned; he joked; he reported late for games; he missed trains, and often he didn't even know the name of the team he was pitching against. However, his mysterious age eventually brought about his downfall as a big leaguer. When he was released by the major leagues, it was believed that he was crowding sixty.

When ageless Satchel Paige was no longer wanted as a pitcher in the major leagues, he still wasn't yet done with pro hurling. He returned to barnstorming, and he continued to pitch and win, in diamond play for money. When he finally quit, he had completed almost a half-century of continuous professional pitching.

In 1971, big-league baseball's conscience was finally stirred sufficiently to honor this genuine American folk hero with official recognition as a diamond immortal. For by then, so towering and awesome a pitching figure was old Satchel Paige, that he was enshrined in the Hall of Fame at Cooperstown. Posterity will remember Leroy (Satchel) Paige, for he blazed the trail to the big leagues for all black hurlers, and he left behind him a most unbelievable pitching record for all baseball players to marvel at.

MANAGERS

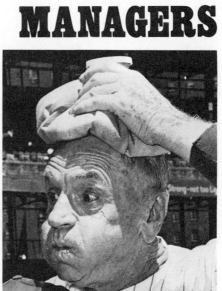

JOHN McGRAW

NAPOLEON IN A DUGOUT

BORN: John Joseph McGraw
      April 7, 1873, Truxton, New York
DIED: February 25, 1934, New Rochelle, New York
HEIGHT: 5'7"   WEIGHT: 150 lbs.
Threw and batted left-handed
Lifetime average (16 years): .334
Record as manager: 10 National League pennants

I n 1902, the New York Giants club was owned by a baseball man named Andrew Freedman who was a politically powerful millionaire, an ignorant brawling bully, and the most despised club owner in the big leagues. He harried his ballplayers, vilified the umpires, fought with fans, and abused his managers as he hired and fired them at will. During his ownership, the New York club, a once-valuable league property, disintegrated into a bedraggled chronic loser in the National League.

However, in the Giants' darkest era, club owner Freedman made one singularly wise and intelligent move that not only greatly benefited baseball, but also enriched the game with an illustrious personality who created a legend of greatness that will live through the ages.

In the middle of that major-league campaign of 1902, with the Giants in last place and sinking rapidly, Freedman hired John McGraw to manage his team. Soon after, Andrew Freedman was forced to sell out and leave major-league baseball forever. But John

McGraw remained to pilot the New York Giants for the next thirty consecutive years, and became the greatest, the most fabulous, and the most world-famous big-league manager of all time.

McGraw was twenty-nine years old when he became the skipper of the Giants. He had been as fine a third baseman as ever played the game. Born in Truxton, New York, the son of a poor Irish railroad worker, he had a most unhappy boyhood. He was only twelve when his mother and four of her children died of diphtheria within a few weeks' time. Grief turned his father into a mean and angry drunkard who often beat John unmercifully. The unhappy boy found escape from his misery in the game of baseball. He would walk miles for a chance to play in a baseball game.

He was barely sixteen when he began playing professional baseball for fame and fortune. By age eighteen, he was playing for the most famous big-league team of his time, the legendary Baltimore Orioles. Small and wiry, weighing hardly 150 lbs., McGraw was a scrappy, quick-thinking, spitfire guardian at the hot corner of the infield. A sure-handed fielder, a speed demon on the base paths, smart and tricky, little Johnny McGraw was also a dangerous .300-plus left-handed hitter. In 1899, he compiled a .390 batting average, which to this day is still the highest ever achieved by a third baseman. He wound up with a lifetime batting average of .334 and the honor of being the most pugnacious player and the most vicious umpire-baiter of his time.

Almost from the start, McGraw revealed a capacity for diamond leadership. Eventually, he became the player-manager of the Orioles. But his incredible saga as baseball's greatest manager really began when he became pilot of the New York Giants. He set a fantastic pace for all other big-league managers to follow.

They nicknamed him the Little Napoleon and he played the part to the hilt. He became the epitome of the supreme baseball dictator. He could swagger sitting down. In the dugout he always towered above all his players because he sat in a specially built raised seat that looked like a throne. He ruled his players with an iron hand, did all their thinking for them, and made all the decisions in every ball game. He glorified or discarded his players according to his whims. Although many of his players hated him for being a diamond martinet, nevertheless almost all major-league players longed to play for him. For he was an unexcelled talent developer. No other manager in history ever had so many of his players gain Hall of Fame immortality as did tough John McGraw. Many of his players became big-league managers in their own right. At one time, almost every club in the two major leagues was piloted by one of McGraw's former players, all imitating his strategy, his pet plays, and his training methods.

In less than two years after he had become the manager of the Giants, he changed that chronic loser into a pennant winner. In 1904, when he won his first pennant, Little Napoleon created an unprecedented furor that shook the major leagues to its roots—he refused to pilot his team in the World Series. He did not think that the American League pennant winner, the Boston Red Sox, was a good enough team to play against his mighty Giants for the baseball championship of the world. Hence, there was no World Series played that year because of John McGraw's decision.

However, as the seasons went by, he won many other pennants — ten in all. No other manager in history ever won more glory than the Little Napoleon of big-league baseball. And only one other pilot ever matched his pennant-winning pace. He was Casey Stengel, who had once played for John McGraw.

During his thirty-year reign as the Giants' manager, little John McGraw became the most colorful, the most dynamic, the most ingenious, the most famous, as well as the most controversial pilot baseball ever had. His influence extended over every facet of major-league activity. He became baseball's ambassador to the world. Out of season, he toured with his players in foreign lands and acquainted the world with the glories of big-league baseball.

As a pacemaker, manager McGraw had no equal. He was the first to give all major-league players dignity in their craft; he changed the face, manners, and style of the game by elevating baseball from its once dingy boardinghouse existence to the luxurious world of swank hotels and multimillion-dollar baseball parks. His effect on major-league baseball was as great as and perhaps even greater than that of any man who was ever connected with the game.

He enriched the game with many startling innovations. He was the first pilot in history to manage a team from the dugout. He was the first to employ and use a pitcher strictly for relief mound duty. Also, he was the first manager to use a pinch hitter in a major-league game and the first to employ a player solely for pinch-hitting duty.

The greatest judge of baseball talent, he bullied, drove, and guided his players to incomparable achievements. In 1916, he piloted his

Giants to seventeen consecutive victories on the road, and before that season ended, to twenty-six triumphs in a row playing at home. Both are still the all-time winning streaks for a major-league team and manager. He won three flags in a row, and he was also the first manager in history to pilot his team to four consecutive pennants, from 1921 through 1924.

In June, 1932, the Little Napoleon, sick and weary, came to the end of his long and glorious reign. He retired from the baseball wars. His sudden departure from the major leagues startled and shocked an entire nation. It was almost unbelievable that John McGraw was no longer the manager of the New York Giants. Two years later he was dead. But he left behind him an incredible record for all big-league managers to match in their dreams of glory. John McGraw did not always win as a major-league manager, but in his thirty years with the Giants he piloted his team to ten pennants, finished second in eleven different seasons, and his teams were in the first division twenty-seven times.

Of all the baseball managers now enshrined in the Hall of Fame, John J. McGraw still towers above all. For his was the legend of the greatest dugout skipper baseball ever had. Baseball historians still speak his name with reverence.

CASEY STENGEL

HALF A CENTURY OF LAUGHS

BORN: Charles Dillon Stengel
July 30, 1889, Kansas City, Missouri
HEIGHT: 5'10"   WEIGHT: 175 lbs.
Threw and batted left-handed
Lifetime average as player (14 years): .284
Record as manager: 1,926 victories and 10 pennants

Casey Stengel was one of the most paradoxical and unbelievable baseball characters. He came to the big leagues when he was twenty-three years old, and he was seventy-five when he finally left the majors. Between his coming and going, he created a never-to-be-forgotten saga of an incomparable buffoon, clown, baseball genuis, and the greatest roving ambassador of goodwill America's national pastime had ever seen.

He became a professional baseball player in his youth in order to earn the money he needed to pay for his schooling as a dentist. But too soon he discovered that the future was not rosy for a left-handed tooth-yanker. So, he turned to playing pro baseball full time to eke out a living.

After rattling around in the obscurity of the minors for a few years, Casey Stengel finally came to the big leagues at the tail end of the 1912 season. The old Brooklyn Dodgers had bought him for five hundred dollars as an outfielder. No other player in history ever made a stranger entrance into the big leagues than Casey Stengel did.

135

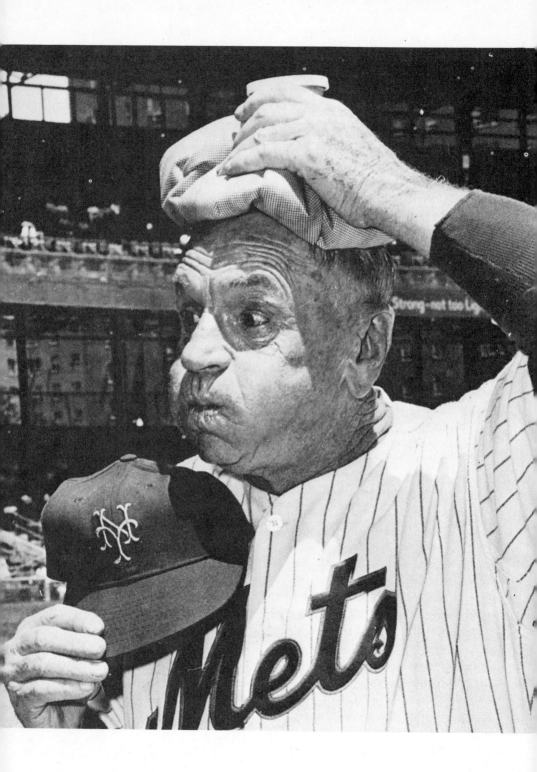

He reported to the Brooklyn Dodgers carrying all his worldly possessions in a shabby paper suitcase, and his entire fortune of ninety-five dollars was pinned to his underwear.

When he found his way into the Dodgers' locker room none of the players paid any attention to him for they were engaged in a dice game. Unknown rookie Casey Stengel joined the game and he quickly lost his entire bankroll.

Before he could get over the shock of his first misfortune in the big leagues, he was jolted by another surprise. The Dodger manager walked in, spotted him, and snapped at him: "You the rookie Stengel? Find yourself a uniform. I'm starting you in center field in this afternoon's game."

Garbed in an ill-fitting baseball uniform, and without even having one day's practice as a major-league outfielder, Casey Stengel staged a spectacular and memorable debut. For in five times at bat, he made four hits, walked once, and also stole two bases. In the outfield, he made several sensational game-saving catches.

With such an astonishing beginning, the reformed dentist quickly found the road to glory as a major-league player. While not becoming the best outfielder in the game, he did distinguish himself as the funniest baseball clown of his time. For fourteen years while starring for five different major-league teams and helping two of them win pennants, Casey Stengel spiced his playing career with more frolic, turmoil, and kookie antics than any other player of his time. His screwball capers and escapades were many and legendary. Nevertheless, clowning and ever-wisecracking Casey completed his fourteen-season career in the majors with appearances in 1,277 games, and collected 1,219 hits for a .284 lifetime batting average.

When his hilarious playing days in the major leagues were over, the celebrated clown Casey proved that he was canny as a fox. For he turned to managing in organized baseball, and for an incredible span of four decades, Casey was never out of a job as a baseball manager, in either the majors or the minors. He piloted nine different baseball clubs.

However, his first two flings as a big-time manager were marred by failure. When he piloted the Brooklyn Dodgers, clowning and wisecracking Casey Stengel "had a ball" with that downtrodden team of mediocre players, screwballs and kooks. But Casey never lost his zest for laughs, even though he clowned himself out of his first job as a major-league pilot.

When he became the manager of another misfit and downtrodden big-league team, the old Boston Braves, again Casey clowned himself out of his job as a major-league pilot. But he never stopped laughing, wisecracking, and clowning.

He was nearing sixty when, in 1949, he hooked on to the most coveted managerial position in the arena of big-league baseball. He became the pilot of the then-fabulous New York Yankees. Everyone was startled and amused. No one expected anything more from Casey than fun and laughs. But the aged buffoon and clown showed what he really could do as a major-league manager with proper diamond talent. For what he accomplished with the Yankees as their pilot for twelve years was to create the most successful and most incredible managerial winning record of all time.

Casey became the first and only manager in major-league history to pilot a team to five consecutive pennants, and five World Series championships in a row. In a fabulous twelve-year span, he piloted the New York Yankees to ten American League pennants, and seven World Series championships. It was the greatest winning feat ever achieved by a major-league manager.

Universal became Casey Stengel's fame as a distinguished and unique big-league pilot. With his warmth, wit, humor, and wisecracks, he became the greatest roving ambassador of goodwill big league baseball ever had. He also became the highest-paid major-league manager in history, a celebrated American citizen, and a millionaire in his own right.

When he was seventy years old, manager Casey Stengel experienced a slight humiliation. The ungrateful New York Yankees fired him as their pilot, because he had grown too old. But he shrugged it off with a laugh and a wisecrack, and quickly found himself another job as a big-league manager. He helped start a new major-league team in the National League — the New York Mets. He became their pilot.

But old Casey found himself saddled and burdened with the most ludicrous baseball team in modern major-league history. While unhappy Casey humorously kept wailing: "Can't anybody around here play baseball?" — his mediocre, befuddled and bewildered Met players lost almost 500 major-league games, in the span of only a few seasons. Nevertheless, manager Stengel made the downtrodden New York Mets the most popular and best-loved baseball team in the major leagues. More people flocked to the ball parks to watch

Casey's funny Met team lose games than went to see the greatest teams in baseball win games. Casey's clowns became the favorite big-league team for the masses.

He continued as a major-league manager until the eve of his seventy-fifth birthday, when he suffered a misfortune that ended his career as a big-league pilot. He fell and broke his hip. Doctors warned him against going on as a baseball manager, and his wife persuaded him to retire from the game. Casey Stengel left the majors with 1,928 victories as a pilot, and a record for winning pennants and World Series championships which will never be eclipsed.

Even after he closed his fantastic fifty-four-year career in pro ball as a player and pilot, he still remained a baseball character for the unusual. For only one year later, he made unprecedented baseball history for his final reward in diamond glory. In a special election, the baseball historians voted him into the Hall of Fame, as an immortal of the game.

Thus ended the incredible saga of a left-handed would-be dentist who went right — all the way to the end of the glory road to become a baseball legend in his lifetime.

THINGS HALL OF FAME IMMORTALS DID

In 1871, his first season in the big leagues, Albert Goodwill Spalding pitched 30 complete games and won 20, thereby becoming the first hurler in history to accomplish a 20-game-win season.

William Henry Wright is the father of professional baseball, for he organized and captained the first openly professional team in baseball's history — the Cincinnati Red Stockings.

Wee Willie Keeler was the smallest big-league player in history. He stood only 64 in. tall, and weighed barely 135 lbs. But he was the first ever to hit safely in as many as 44 consecutive major-league games, and finished with a 20-year lifetime batting average of .345.

Michael "King" Kelly was the first glamorous big-league star in history. He was not only the best-dressed big leaguer of the nineteenth century, but for a time he was actually acclaimed by fashion experts in America and Europe as the best-dressed man in the world.

William Billy Hamilton was probably the fastest base-stealer in major-league history. In the 1889 season, he stole 117 bases. Although he played only 14 years he swiped almost a thousand bases.

Wilbert Robinson was for 18 seasons one of the greatest catchers in history. On June 10, 1892, he became the only player in major-league history to make seven safe hits in seven times at bat, during one nine-inning game.

The only player in history who won the batting championship of both major leagues was first baseman Ed Delahanty. In 1899, playing for the Philadelphia Phillies, he hit .408 to win the National League batting title, and in 1902, playing for the Washington Senators, he hit .376 to capture the American League batting crown.

Outfielder Hugh Duffy achieved the highest one-season batting average ever recorded in major-league history. In the 1894 season, playing in 124 games, he hit .438.

Pitcher William "Candy" Cummings is credited with being the inventor of the curve ball.

Outfielder Jesse Cail Burkett was the first big-league player in history to bat .400 a season — three times, 1895, 1896 and 1899. Only two Hall of Famers ever matched this feat.

John "Happy Jack" Chesbro won the most games in a season in modern major-league history. In 1904, he hurled 53 games and he won 41.

Roger Bresnahan was the first catcher in history to wear a chest protector and mask, and he invented shin guards for all backstops to use.

Cornelius McGillicuddy, known as Connie Mack, managed major-league teams longer than any other man in history. His fantastic record stretched over 53 years. He piloted the Philadelphia Athletics for 50 consecutive seasons.

"Iron Man" Joe McGinnity pitched more doubleheaders than any other hurler in major-league history. In August of 1903, he hurled three complete doubleheaders and won all six games.

Left-hander Richard "Rube" Marquard pitched and won the Opening Day game of the 1912 season, and he continued to win until he achieved the longest winning streak ever accomplished by a twentieth century pitcher in one season. He won 19 games in a row.

The pitcher who put together the longest winning streak in all major-league history was Carl Hubbell. Over two seasons (1936–1937) he won 24 games in a row.

Second baseman Eddie Collins who played in the major leagues longer than any other modern star in history (25 years) was the most incredible one-game base stealer of all time. In one game during the 1912 season, he stole six bases. Eleven days later, in another nine-inning game, he again stole six bases.

Charles Augustus "Kid" Nichols was the greatest pitching winner of 30-victory seasons in history. During his 17 years in the big leagues, he hurled 30 or more wins a season seven times.

Outfielders Paul Waner and Lloyd Waner, each only 68 in. tall, and famed as "Big Poison" and "Little Poison," are the only real brothers in the Hall of Fame. Between them, the Waner Brothers collected 5,611 safe hits in major-league play.

First baseman Frank Chance known as the Peerless Leader was the greatest player-manager in history. In less than eight seasons, he piloted the Chicago Cubs to four pennants, and two World Series championships. In 1906, he piloted his team to 116 victories, which is still an unmatched major-league record.

Branch Rickey was the most remarkable innovator in major-league history. He revolutionized big-league baseball and caused significant changes in the game; he reshaped the entire sport. He broke the color line in organized baseball.

James Emory Foxx was one of the game's most versatile players. As a first baseman, catcher, third baseman and outfielder too, he was the strongest man in major-league history. Known as the Beast he hit baseballs harder and further than anyone in history.

Samuel "Wahoo" Crawford collected more three-base hits than any other major-league batsman in history. He hit 312.

Shortstop Joe Cronin commanded the highest price ever paid for one player in a trade between two major-league teams. In 1934, the Washington Senators sold him to the Boston Red Sox for $250,000 in cash. Curiously, the Washington club owner who sold him for that record price was his father-in-law, Clark Griffith.

Although William J. Klem never played big-league baseball, nevertheless, he became the most famous major-league umpire of all time. Known as the Old Arbitrator he invented the behind-the-plate stance that all umpires now use, and he brought dignity and respect to the umpiring profession.

Big Ed Walsh, the best spitball hurler of them all, set the all-time record for innings pitched in one season. In 1908, he hurled 464 innings for the Chicago White Sox and won 40 games.

Pitcher Charles "Red" Ruffing is the only immortal in the Hall of Fame minus four toes on his left foot. He overcame the misfortune of a mine accident in his youth and became a major-league winner of 273 games.

Charles "Chief" Bender is the only American Indian in the Hall of Fame. A member of the Chippewa tribe, he was regarded as the greatest clutch pitcher in history. In his 15 years in the majors, he won more than 200 games and 6 World Series games.

On September 16, 1924, in a game against the old Brooklyn Dodgers, first baseman Jim (Sunny) Bottomley of the St. Louis Cardinals made 6 hits in 6 times at bat, and drove in 12 runs, to set an RBI-record for a single major-league game that has never been equaled.

Vernon "Lefty" Gomez, who was known as "Goofy" during his glorious pitching years in the major leagues because of his clowning and kooky eccentricities, set an all-time World Series mark as a perfect pitcher. He hurled 6 games without a loss.

Early Wynn set a longevity record as a big-league pitcher. He hurled in the majors for 23 years, winning 300 games.

Lou Boudreau, an All-American college basketball star, became not only one of the greatest big-league shortstops of all time, but also the youngest major-league manager in history. When he became the player-manager of the Cleveland Indians back in the 1940s, he was only 24 years old.

Pud Galvin was the first pitcher in major-league history to win 300 games.

Joe McCarthy was the winningest manager of all major-league time. In his 24 years as a big-league pilot, his teams compiled a lofty .614 won-lost percentage, while capturing 9 pennants and finishing second 7 times. He was the first manager in history to win a pennant in each of the two major leagues. Curiously, he never had been good enough to make the big leagues as a player.

FIRST BASEMEN	Period	G	AB	R	H	RBI	Pct.
Anson, Cap	1876–1897	2253	9084	1712	3081	1715	.339
Beckley, Jake	1888–1907	2373	9476	1601	2930	1575	.309
Brouthers, Dan	1879–1904	1658	6725	1507	2349	1056	.349
Chance, Frank	1898–1914	1232	4279	796	1273	596	.297
Foxx, Jimmie	1925–1945	2317	8134	1751	2646	1921	.325
Gehrig, Lou	1923–1939	2164	8001	1888	2721	1991	.340
Greenberg, Hank	1930–1947	1394	5193	1051	1628	1276	.313
Kelly, George	1915–1932	1622	5993	819	1778	1019	.297
Sisler, George	1915–1930	2055	8267	1284	2812	1180	.340
Terry, Bill	1923–1936	1721	6428	1120	2193	1078	.341
SECOND BASEMEN							
Collins, Eddie	1906–1930	2825	9949	1819	3312	1307	.333
Evers, Johnny	1902–1929	1776	6136	919	1659	538	.270
Frisch, Frank	1919–1937	2311	9112	1532	2880	1242	.316
Gehringer, Charlie	1924–1942	2323	8860	1773	2839	1427	.320
Hornsby, Rogers	1915–1937	2259	8173	1579	2930	1579	.358
Lajoie, Nap	1896–1916	2475	9589	1503	3251	1599	.339
Robinson, Jackie	1947–1956	1382	4877	947	1518	734	.311
SHORTSTOPS							
Appling, Luke	1930–1950	2422	8857	1319	2749	1116	.310
Bancroft, Dave	1915–1930	1913	7182	1048	2004	579	.279
Boudreau, Lou	1938–1952	1646	6030	861	1779	789	.295
Cronin, Joe	1926–1945	2124	7577	1233	2285	1423	.302
Jennings, Hugh	1891–1918	1264	4840	989	1520	840	.314
Maranville, Rabbit	1912–1935	2670	10078	1255	2605	874	.258
Tinker, Joe	1902–1916	1642	5936	716	1565	783	.264
Wagner, Honus	1897–1917	2785	10427	1740	3430	1732	.329
Wallace, Bobby	1894–1918	2369	8629	1056	2308	1121	.267
Ward, Monte	1878–1894	1810	7579	1403	2151	—	.283
THIRD BASEMEN							
Baker, Frank	1908–1922	1575	5985	887	1838	1012	.307
Collins, Jimmy	1895–1908	1718	6792	1057	1999	985	.294
Traynor, Pie	1920–1937	1941	7559	1183	2416	1273	.320
LEFT FIELDERS							
Burkett, Jesse	1890–1905	2063	8389	1708	2872	952	.342
Clarke, Fred	1894–1915	2204	8584	1620	2703	1015	.315
Delahanty, Ed	1888–1903	1825	7493	1596	2593	1464	.346
Goslin, Goose	1921–1938	2287	8654	1483	2735	1609	.316
Hafey, Chick	1924–1937	1283	4625	777	1466	833	.317
Kelley, Joe	1891–1908	1827	6982	1424	2244	1194	.321
Medwick, Joe	1932–1948	1984	7635	1198	2471	1383	.324
Musial, Stan	1941–1963	3026	10972	1949	3630	1951	.331
O'Rourke, Jim	1876–1904	1750	7365	1425	2314	—	.314
Simmons, Al	1924–1944	2215	8761	1507	2927	1827	.334
Wheat, Zack	1909–1927	2406	9106	1289	2884	1265	.317
Williams, Ted	1939–1960	2292	7706	1798	2654	1839	.344
CENTER FIELDERS							
Carey, Max	1910–1929	2469	9363	1545	2665	797	.285
Cobb, Ty	1905–1928	3034	11437	2245	4192	1954	.367
Combs, Earle	1924–1935	1455	5748	1186	1866	629	.325
Cuyler, Kiki	1921–1938	1879	7161	1305	2299	1065	.321
DiMaggio, Joe	1936–1951	1736	6821	1390	2214	1537	.325
Duffy, Hugh	1888–1906	1722	6999	1545	2307	1299	.330
Hamilton, Billy	1888–1901	1578	6262	1690	2157	736	.344
Mantle, Mickey	1951–1968	2401	8102	1677	2415	1500	.298
Roush, Edd	1913–1931	1748	6646	1001	2158	882	.325
Speaker, Tris	1907–1928	2789	10208	1881	3515	1559	.344
Waner, Lloyd	1927–1945	1993	7772	1201	2459	598	.316

BERS OF THE HALL OF FAME

RIGHT FIELDERS	Period	G	AB	R	H	RBI	Pct.
Clemente, Roberto	1955–1972	2433	9454	1416	3000	1305	.317
Crawford, Sam	1899–1917	2505	9579	1392	2964	1525	.309
Flick, Elmer	1898–1910	1480	5597	948	1764	756	.315
Heilmann, Harry	1914–1932	2146	7787	1291	2660	1549	.342
Hooper, Harry	1909–1925	2308	8784	1429	2466	813	.281
Keeler, Willie	1892–1910	2124	8564	1720	2955	810	.345
Manush, Heinie	1923–1939	2009	7653	1287	2524	1173	.330
McCarthy, Tommy	1884–1896	1258	5055	1050	1485	—	.294
Ott, Mel	1926–1947	2730	9456	1859	2876	1860	.304
Rice, Sam	1915–1934	2404	9269	1515	2987	1077	.322
Ruth, Babe	1914–1935	2503	8399	2174	2873	2209	.342
Waner, Paul	1926–1945	2549	9459	1626	3152	1309	.333
Youngs, Ross	1917–1926	1211	4627	812	1491	596	.322

CATCHERS							
Berra, Yogi	1946–1965	2120	7555	1175	2150	1430	.285
Bresnahan, Roger	1897–1915	1410	4480	684	1251	531	.279
Campanella, Roy	1948–1957	1215	4205	627	1161	856	.276
Cochrane, Mickey	1925–1937	1482	5169	1041	1652	832	.320
Dickey, Bill	1928–1946	1789	6300	930	1969	1209	.313
Ewing, Buck	1880–1897	1281	5348	1118	1663	—	.311
Hartnett, Gabby	1922–1941	1990	6432	867	1912	1179	.297
Kelly, King	1878–1893	1434	5922	1359	1853	—	.313
Schalk, Ray	1912–1929	1760	5306	579	1345	596	.253

PITCHERS	Period	G	IP	Won	Lost	Pct.
Alexander, Grover	1911–1930	696	5189	373	208	.642
Bender, Chief	1903–1925	459	3026	212	128	.624
Brown, Mordecai	1903–1916	481	3168	239	130	.631
Chesbro, Jack	1899–1909	392	2886	198	127	.609
Clarkson, John	1882–1894	517	4514	327	176	.650
Coveleski, Stan	1912–1928	450	3092	216	142	.603
Dean, Dizzy	1930–1947	317	1966	150	83	.644
Faber, Red	1914–1933	669	4087	254	212	.545
Feller, Bob	1936–1956	570	3828	266	162	.621
Ford, Whitey	1950–1967	498	3171	236	106	.690
Galvin, Pud	1879–1892	675	5959	361	309	.539
Gomez, Lefty	1930–1943	368	2503	189	102	.649
Grimes, Burleigh	1916–1934	.615	4178	270	212	.560
Grove, Lefty	1925–1941	616	3940	300	140	.682
Haines, Jess	1918–1937	555	3207	210	158	.571
Hoyt, Waite	1918–1938	674	3762	237	182	.566
Hubbell, Carl	1928–1943	535	3591	253	154	.622
Johnson, Walter	1907–1927	802	5924	416	279	.599
Keefe, Tim	1880–1893	599	5050	344	225	.605
Koufax, Sandy	1955–1966	397	2325	165	87	.655
Lyons, Ted	1923–1946	594	4162	260	230	.531
Marquard, Rube	1908–1925	536	3307	201	177	.532
Mathewson, Christy	1900–1916	635	4781	373	188	.665
McGinnity, Joe	1899–1908	467	3455	247	145	.630
Nichols, Kid	1890–1906	582	5067	360	202	.641
Pennock, Herb	1912–1934	617	3558	240	162	.597
Plank, Eddie	1901–1917	623	4503	326	192	.629
Radbourne, Old Hoss	1880–1891	517	4543	308	191	.617
Rixey, Eppa	1912–1933	692	4494	266	251	.515
Ruffing, Red	1924–1947	624	4342	273	225	.548
Spahn, Warren	1942–1965	750	5246	363	245	.597
Vance, Dazzy	1915–1935	442	2967	197	140	.585
Waddell, Rube	1897–1910	407	2958	191	142	.574
Walsh, Ed	1904–1917	431	2968	195	126	.607
Welch, Mickey	1880–1892	565	4783	308	209	.596
Wynn, Early	1939–1963	691	4566	300	244	.551
Young, Cy	1890–1911	906	7377	511	313	.620

145

MANAGERS	Period	Won	Lost
Huggins, Miller	1913–1929	1413	1134
Mack, Connie	1894–1950	3776	4025
McCarthy, Joe	1926–1950	2126	1335
McGraw, John	1899–1932	2840	1984
McKechnie, Bill	1915–1946	1898	1724
Robinson, Wilbert	1902–1931	1397	1395
Stengel, Casey	1934–1965	1926	1867

UMPIRES	Years
Jocko Conlan	24
Tommy Connolly	30
Billy Evans	22
Bill Klem	35

FOR MERITORIOUS SERVICE TO BASEBALL

Edward Barrow	Executive
Morgan G. Bulkeley	Executive
Alexander Cartwright	Pioneer
Henry Chadwick	Writer–Statistician
William Cummings	Inventor of Curve Ball
Ford Frick	Baseball Commissioner
William Harridge	League President
Bancroft Johnson	League President
Kenesaw Mountain Landis	First Baseball Commissioner
Branch Rickey	Executive
Albert G. Spalding	Pioneer–Pitcher
George Weiss	Executive
George Wright	Pioneer–Player
Harry Wright	Pioneer–Manager

NEGRO BASEBALL LEAGUES IMMORTALS

James (Cool Papa) Bell	Outfielder
Josh Gibson	Catcher
Monte Irvin	Infielder–Outfielder
Walter Leonard	First Baseman
Leroy (Satchel) Paige	Pitcher

ABOUT THE AUTHOR

MAC DAVIS is widely known as a sports storyteller. Readers of his twenty previous sports books number well up in the millions. But many more sports fans have heard his fascinating stories broadcast over hundreds of radio stations throughout the United States, Canada, and Europe. He has created and written many popular sports shows presented on the air and hosted by many of America's most famous sportscasters.